HotTips for Facilitators

Strategies to Make Life Easier
for Anyone Who Leads, Guides,
Teaches, or Trains Groups

ROB ABERNATHY and MARK REARDON

Zephyr Press

Chicago

HotTips for Facilitators
Strategies to Make Life Easier for Anyone Who Leads, Guides,
Teaches, or Trains Groups

© 2003 by Rob Abernathy and Mark Reardon

Printed in the United States of America

ISBN-13: 978-1-56976-150-2
ISBN-10: 1-56976-150-7

Cover design: Rattray Design
Cover image: © Photodisc, C Squared Studios

Published by
Zephyr Press
An imprint of Chicago Review Press, Incorporated
814 North Franklin Street
Chicago, Illinois 60610
(800) 232-2187
www.zephyrpress.com

Library of Congress Cataloging-in-Publication Data

Abernathy, Rob, 1953–
  HotTips for facilitators : strategies to make life easier for anyone
who leads, guides, teaches, or trains groups / Rob Abernathy and
Mark Reardon.
    p. cm.
Includes bibliographical references.
  ISBN 1-56976-150-7
Group facilitation. I. Title: Hot tips for facilitators. II.
Reardon, Mark, 1957– III. Title.
  HM751 .A24 2002
  302.3'4—dc21   2002007390

*W*e dedicate this book to our newest borns: Bryce David Abernathy and Tate Macrae Reardon. To Bryce David Abernathy, the joy-giver in the Abernathy household. You bring to our lives an innocent and fresh outlook at the wonder of fully exploring every moment of life. You're the best! To Tate Macrae Reardon, my cheerful son of grace. You touch a joyful place in my heart and remind me of the wonder of creation. Thank you!

Acknowledgments

This book is a compilation of what we have found to be useful. We have borrowed, modified, and created based on the modeling and input of people we admire and respect. Among the many who have influenced both what we know and what we do, we wish to specifically acknowledge the following: Rich Allen, Suzanne Bailey, Brian Blackstock, Robin and Kathy Bocchino, Betty Edwards, Robert Garmston, Michael Grinder, Madeline Hunter, Eric Jensen, Michael Kaufman, Kate Neale, Gabriele Rico, Blair Singer, Michael Wall, and The Learning Teams at Grossmont Union High School District and Fallbrook Union Elementary School District.

About the Authors

Rob Abernathy is recognized as being among the top trainers in the United States. Currently CEO of Intertrainment, a consulting firm that sponsors seminars on curriculum development, accountability in education, and assessment issues, Abernathy previously worked for the Orange County Department of Education and the Orange County, California, School Leadership Academy, facilitating a variety of training experiences for educators. He holds a master's degree in educational administration from Azuza Pacific University, as well as administrative, special education, and multiple-subject teaching credentials. He is coauthor of the HotTips series.

Mark Reardon is president of Centre Pointe Education, culminating twenty-two years of experience as a teacher, principal, and educational consultant. Throughout his career, his focus has remained on discovering what works in teaching and learning. Drawing on his bachelor's degree in psychology from California Lutheran University and his master's degree in educational administration from California State University, Fullerton, Reardon translates learning theory into understandable, usable practices for educators. He has taught learners of all ages, from children to university professors, parents to CEOs. His expertise encompasses professional development, train-the-trainer seminars, communication and team-building skills, as well as curriculum and program design. He is coauthor of *Quantum Teaching: Orchestrating Student Success* and the HotTips series.

Contents

About This Book

We wrote this book to provide teachers, administrators, trainers, and presenters with strategies for effective facilitation. According to the *New Oxford Dictionary of English, facilitate* means "to make easy or easier" (by process or means). Effective facilitation, then, involves using strategies and techniques to make the learning process easier. We believe it is possible to enhance people's learning by improving the way we facilitate the process. The tips in this book can help you facilitate, "make easy," the classes, meetings, workshops, or seminars you lead.

What Is a Facilitator?

Isn't *facilitator* just another word for teacher, administrator, trainer, or presenter? Not really. Whenever you attempt to "make easy" the learning process, you assume the role of facilitator. Facilitators guide people as they plan, problem-solve, and learn. It is a vastly dynamic endeavor. Teachers, administrators, trainers, and presenters may all act as facilitators at various times, in various settings.

With some adaptation, these tips are applicable to a range of adult and child learners in a variety of settings: a classroom, workshop, business meeting, or in-service, for example. It's difficult to find a generic term that covers such a range of people. We have chosen *participant* to refer to the student, workshop attendee, meeting attendee, or other person you may facilitate. As you read, consider how you might implement each HotTip most effectively in your situation. Enjoy making these strategies and your learning environment come alive.

What Are HotTips?

HotTips are a collection of strategies that have worked for us, have worked for our friends, and will work for you. In this book you will find proven theories, tools, strategies, and techniques for designing, facilitating, and debriefing experiences in the classroom and the conference room. HotTips are adaptable to your style and your situation, and they get results. You will find that some of the HotTips are related. For example, Plan Fingertip Questions, Ask Two Powerful Questions, and Do the "Now How" all assist in planning and guiding discussions. Similarly, Create Storyboards and Ride the Brainstorm Carousel are useful for generating and organizing ideas.

In offering these tips we in no way wish to suggest that facilitation can be reduced to a mere set of duplicable tricks. Indeed, we honor the dynamic interactions that occur during facilitation. We realize that facilitation based solely on tools or techniques is insufficient to produce enduring change. Premier facilitators use these tools and techniques to ignite the inspiration and passion within the hearts of their participants. In the process, they not only assist the group in accomplishing the task at hand, but re-energize them as well. As you employ these HotTips, bear in mind, as we do, the awesome complexities of the transformative work we all do.

What Is a HotTips Book and How Is It Organized?

A HotTips book is

- an effective tool that makes learning and information come alive through interactive text and activities.
- an artfully designed workbook with space for you to record your thoughts, writings, and personal interactions with the material.
- an information-to-knowledge-to-application tool that provides relevant, brain-friendly, and immediately applicable strategies.
- a collection of innovative and foundational information that will enhance your effectiveness as a communicator, whether you are facilitating a small group or lecturing in a giant hall.

This HotTips book will enhance your skill integration and implementation. It will amplify your natural abilities by helping you tap into your knowledge, experience, and creativity while capitalizing on brain-compatible learning strategies. The activities take you beyond information to integration and application. As you work with the design, you will experience the way it becomes smart, relevant, and useful. The more actively you engage yourself with the activities and applications, the more valuable the book becomes.

We begin with ways of thinking—internal scaffolds on which to build facilitation savvy. Design with Them in Mind reminds us to place the participants and what they want (or need) to accomplish in the spotlight. "It's always about them" is a guiding principle of any effective facilitator. Know How They Are Smart reminds us that participants possess an array of intelligences waiting to be amplified. Capture Collective Capacities reassures us that participants know more than they think they do. Remind, Don't Rescue advises us to allow participants to experience challenging moments during the process. As a context piece, That Was Then, This Is Now helps participants understand the expectations of them in a new experience. Anticipate the Next Move empowers us to be constantly thinking ahead. Ride the Winds of Fate, Call an Audible, and Plan Fingertip Questions are tips used to keep the learning process on track when the unexpected happens. Pause, Be Silent, and Attend; Every Body Tells a Story; and Know Their Hearts enhance our ability to stay connected with participants during the meeting or training. Celebrate Resistance offers ideas for responding proactively to challenging participants, while Take Exits, On-Ramps, and Segues provides phrases and sentences for smooth transitions.

We continue the book with processes and activities. Create KnowBooks and Other Graphic Organizers explores ways for participants to record their insights and knowledge. Take a Page brings out participants' assumptions. Ask Two Powerful Questions and Do the "Now How" provide useful questions for facilitating systemic change. Create Storyboards and Ride the Brainstorm Carousel are structured idea- and solution-generating activities. To assist participants in moving through challenging situations, we offer Solve Problems with Dimensioning. Use the Classics contains three activities designed to enhance teamwork and group exploration. We wrap up the book with Debrief Their Learning, which leads you through the all-important concluding moments of an experiential activity, followed by Walk about to Facilitate Reflection and Growth, a self-reflective strategy to help you improve your facilitation ability.

Page 5 previews the layout of this HotTips book and how you will use it. All but three of the HotTips follow the same format, with icons to guide you to specific information. The three activities in Use the Classics follow a lesson plan format, which better suits their structure. Each section title is the name of a HotTip. Although we have attempted to group the tips logically, the order does not necessarily reflect the order in which you will utilize the tips nor their relative importance.

So grab a colored pen or pencil, or perhaps a highlighter. Read over these HotTips. Make them yours. Leave your fingerprints on these pages through your symbols, words, color, and reflective thoughts. Then feel the impact of each HotTip during your next facilitation experience. And, whatever you do, facilitate like it matters!

Also look for more books in the HotTips series. *HotTips for Teachers* is full of handy tips to help teachers hold students' attention and maximize learning. And *HotTips for Speakers* gives you ideas for making every public speaking engagement memorable.

Reflecting on Effective Facilitation

You might be wondering what distinguishes facilitation from teaching, administrating, training, or presenting. Here are a few characteristics of effective facilitators:

- Facilitators guide the interaction and participants' acquisition of knowledge, skills, and ideas, rather than simply delivering knowledge, skills, and ideas. This is usually done through a group process.
- Facilitators empower participants through purposeful design, elegant guidance, and wise discernment.
- Facilitators orchestrate problem solving and learning using impeccable designs that lead participants to reflection and discovery.
- Facilitators operate from an overarching goal and a vision of what's possible during the event.
- Facilitators rely on intuition and acuity. Their ability to "read the room" is well developed.

The HotTip is defined in an action phrase that distills its essence in easily remembered language.

Making It Mine is designed specifically to guide implementation. It contains brain-compatible learning strategies that help you cement the HotTip into your repertoire. This section will take you well on your way toward mastery!

Thinking It Over provides a place to reflect on what you have learned. If you are too busy to reflect, you are too busy to grow. Think about it!

Between the quotation marks is an affirmation designed to strengthen your internal beliefs. Say this thought often.

- Facilitators guide the process, moving from the known to the unknown, making decisions and changes in response to participants' needs.
- Facilitators "make easy" the process of learning, guiding the group toward a shared destination.

Guiding Principles

Facilitators employ guiding principles or beliefs that govern their decisions, and undoubtedly you already possess such a set. We share the following principles both as a place to start and to allow you to compare your presuppositions with the ones that underlie this book.

1. **The truth is out there:** Facilitators believe that participants are smart and possess potential. Many of us find it easy to tell others what to do and to give advice. Advice—especially when unsolicited—is not facilitative. Effective facilitators recognize that all participants are perfect just the way they are, and that they often have more knowledge and understanding than they give themselves credit for. The values of respect, honor, accomplishment, fulfillment, and integrity compose the bedrock of effective facilitation. Time, patience, acuity, and a relentless pursuit of possibilities drive the facilitator outward to find the truth resident in the participants.

2. **Participants are on a journey:** Facilitators believe that the role of the participant is that of discoverer, traveler, detective, and explorer. The learning process is not ours, it's theirs. Our role as facilitator is to make the participants' journey as easy and memorable as possible. As participants uncover a deeper understanding of what they already know, or integrate and synthesize what they already know with new refinements, facilitators guide the journey. Guiding the learning process takes a certain amount of fearlessness in the midst of uncertainty. It requires that you have sufficient self-awareness to realize you don't have the answers, and really might not know how you and the group are going to accomplish the task ahead. Even though you have a tool bag of skills and a plan for the learning experience, facilitation takes a willingness to flow with the process and respond to feedback from participants. It requires that you tap into the collective genius of the group and the creativity

of each participant. Facilitation is moment-by-moment adjustment mixed with a keen sense of purpose and direction and a dose of wide-eyed wonder.

3. **The design is just a map:** Facilitators believe that the map is not the territory. A map is a pictorial representation of the general terrain. But once you get to the actual spot shown on a map, it is much easier to ascertain the landscape. To be effective facilitators we never forget that our best designs are just that: *ours*. Even with years of experience and keen acuity, we cannot anticipate and plan for every situation. Only during the actual learning experience with our participants does the path fully emerge. This principle reminds us that we have to be willing to modify even our best-laid plans.

4. **Facilitators make participants' knowledge and schemas conscious:** Facilitators believe that their role is not to persuade but rather to make conscious. Through careful design, appropriately interjected questions, and well-designed scenarios, facilitators assist participants in becoming conscious of their mental models and daily practices. There is no need to persuade others when you can let them persuade themselves!

5. **Feedback equals results:** Facilitators know that two ingredients are crucial to obtaining desired results: state and context. Facilitators routinely analyze the results they receive: Did I get the result I was expecting or not? If not, why not? If so, why? What state of mind were participants in during the activity? How did the directions (the context) influence their state of mind and thereby the result?

6. **Celebrate the wonder:** Above all, facilitators are constantly mindful of learning's wondrous dynamics. Learning is complex, fluid, and sprinkled with sudden insights that illuminate the mind like fireworks on a clear evening.

It is from this set of guiding principles that we offer strategies and models we have found to be effective time and time again.

Making This Book Mine

As you start, here are a few reflective questions to accelerate your growth:

As a facilitator, do I draw on participants' prior knowledge, helping them to see the connections between what they already know and the new information? How and why do I do so?

_____

_____

As a facilitator, how do I use a variety of instructional strategies and resources to respond to my participants' diverse needs? Why do I do so?

_____

_____

As a facilitator, how do I design learning experiences that provide opportunities for independent and collaborative learning? Why do I do so?

_____

_____

As a facilitator, how do I engage participants in problem solving, critical thinking, and other activities that make the content and ideas meaningful? Why do I do so?

_____

_____

As a facilitator, how do I promote self-directed, reflective learning for all participants? Why do I do so?

_____

_____

This book is about you and your development as a productive, discerning, savvy, and competent facilitator. Let's begin!

Part 1

Maximize Learning

The moment when learning occurs is crucial. We have known for years how important that moment is, how the quality of that moment influences our perception of the event. Imagine if you could orchestrate those moments, perhaps even design for them so that learning could be maximized.

This section begins with the design of facilitated experiences and asks you to anticipate the dynamics of those who will attend, their learning outcomes, their learning styles, their questions and concerns, and even the questions you might ask and how you will keep them on track toward their learning outcomes.

Design with Them in Mind

Use this powerful yet simple design frame for creating a provocative, relevant, and meaningful design for any participant-focused, interactive learning experience.

There are a variety of ways to approach the design of any participant-focused, interactive workshop. Some of us may start with the content, others by identifying the desired outcomes, and still others by creating a Mind Map of all the possible processes and designs. Served up for you in this HotTip is a participant-focused design frame to hold your thoughts and ideas and help you organize that information into a blueprint or agenda for your presentation. *Design with Them in Mind is only one organizer of many.* It is our staple design and the one we use most often. It is simple to navigate, covers all the design bases and questions, and focuses attention on the participants first and foremost. You might call it an "all about them design frame."

Making It Mine

Imagine that late one afternoon you receive a call from the assistant superintendent, who politely requests your services to design and facilitate a workshop with all the district principals the next morning. Or, imagine you are a promising corporate trainer with a Fortune 500 company. A CEO had planned an employee seminar on effective communication. The person who was to conduct the seminar had an emergency, and you have been summoned as the replacement. What do you do? How do you plan for such an event on such short notice?

No problem, my friend, simply use the Design with Them in Mind visual organizer and the following six steps to frame your presentation.

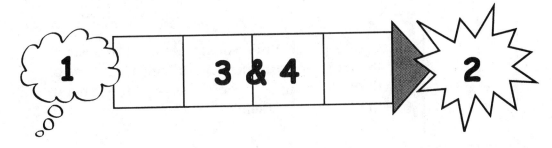

1. Stand in the shoes of your participants. What needs, hopes, concerns, experiences, and burning questions will they bring with them as they walk in the door? From their perspective, what will make the event meaningful, relevant, and powerful?

2. Analyze the larger system. What outcomes and success indicators do you wish to be evident when the event is over? How do you envision the system being better in three or four months as a result of the event?

3. Plan your content. What are the chunks of information or content pieces of your design? You might link the chunks as answers to compelling participant questions or concerns you identified in step 1.

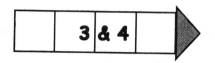

4. In view of participants' learning needs and probable levels of mastery, also consider how much content you will provide them and how long you will allow them to process that information. In our experience, usually about half lecture (content) and half small-group discussion or activities (processing the content) is effective. To maximize behavior shift, include strategies that link the activity to critical organizational issues and plan opportunities for participants to use their bodies in learning.

5. Create a large outline or agenda you can post on the wall to keep participants oriented. List or map the major components of the session and general time frames for them.

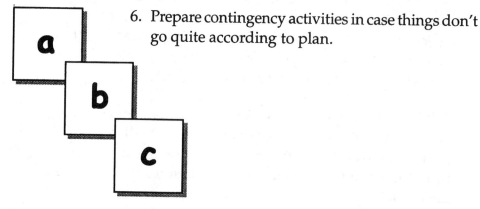

6. Prepare contingency activities in case things don't go quite according to plan.

Thinking It Over

What can I change, add, or delete in the Design with Them in Mind procedure to better fit my personal strengths and current planning process?

_____

_____

_____

_____

What step in this HotTip do I find the easiest to accomplish? The most difficult? What self-improvement strategies could I use to build on my strengths and reduce my weaknesses?

_____

_____

_____

_____

What makes Design with Them in Mind a powerful tool in designing a meeting or facilitation?

_____

_____

_____

_____

> When I Design with Them in Mind, I can quickly plan powerful learning events.

Know How
They Are Smart

Learn how to design and facilitate "brain satisfying" learning environments.

Howard Gardner, in his book *Frames of Mind* (1993), describes his theory of multiple intelligences, or eight "ways of knowing." Each of us possesses these eight intelligences and can use them productively, but in each individual certain intelligences are stronger or preferred over others. By having participants engage in activities that exercise all the intelligences, we can literally hot-wire their brains. Brain research indicates that when we solve problems or learn by exercising underused intelligences, or several intelligences at once, the electrical activity of the brain jumps dramatically. Synapses fire madly and dendrites look for connections. Creativity is enhanced. As facilitators, we have observed that tapping into multiple intelligences exercises the mind and accelerates learning.

Know How They Are Smart is a resource and guide in translating the theory of multiple intelligences into facilitation tools and strategies. The essence of the HotTip is quite simple: In reality there are a multiplicity of ways to be smart. When we recognize that each participant is smart in many ways and has his or her own unique ways of being smart, we end up transforming how we facilitate. We can tap participants' "smart" resources by including diverse approaches to gathering ideas, issues, and information when planning meetings, activities, and learning experiences. We can create smart learning environments by incorporating different ways of engaging participants' "smarts."

The eight different intelligences, or ways of knowing, Howard Gardner has identified are visual-spatial, verbal-linguistic, interpersonal, musical-rhythmic, naturalist, bodily-kinesthetic, intrapersonal, and logical-mathematical. Traditional planning processes tend to focus on the verbal-linguistic, logical-mathematical, and to a lesser extent, interpersonal intelligences.

Making It Mine

The **visual-spatial** participant thinks in images and pictures. How can I amplify participants' sense of sight? How can I use color, art, visual aids, and internal mental imaging?

_____

_____

_____

The **verbal-linguistic** participant thinks in words. How can I incorporate language, written and spoken? How can I use stories, discussions, debates, and probing conversations?

_____

_____

_____

The **interpersonal** participant thinks by communicating with others. How can I engage participants in interpersonal interaction and communication? How can I incorporate collaboration, peer sharing, and group simulations?

_____

_____

_____

The **musical-rhythmic** participant thinks in sounds, rhythms, and tone patterns. How can I include tonal patterns, a variety of environmental music and sounds, and a sensitivity to rhythm? How can I set key points in a rhythmic or melodic framework?

_____

_____

The **naturalist** participant is good at recognizing patterns and categories in the natural world. How can I use products and processes of nature to enhance their learning experience?

_____

_____

The **bodily-kinesthetic** participant thinks and processes through bodily sensations and movement. How can I utilize physical movement to promote muscle memory? How can I use simulation and hands-on activities?

_____

_____

The **intrapersonal** participant thinks through focusing on internal feelings and intuition. How can I tap into participants' inner states of being, self-reflection, and metacognition? How can I evoke emotions and give my participants choices?

_____

_____

The **logical-mathematical** participant thinks conceptually, and is good at recognizing patterns and relationships. How can I orchestrate inductive and deductive thinking and reasoning, and the recognition of abstract patterns? How can I incorporate numbers, calculation, logic, and critical thinking?

_____

_____

Thinking It Over

Since I've been incorporating more intelli-gences into my learning events, what differences have I noticed in my participants?

_____

_____

_____

_____

_____

What do I find the most challenging aspect of designing a more "intelligence-friendly" learning event?

_____

_____

_____

When I facilitate, which intelligences do I consistently favor?

_____

_____

_____

When I facilitate, which intelligences do I seldom if ever tap?

_____

_____

_____

> I create multiple avenues for my participants to maximize their engagement with the content.

Capture Collective Capacities

Facilitate the collective and intellectual capital of your learners.

The art of facilitation begins with this essential belief: Learners know more than they think they do. Our role as facilitators is to help them tap into that knowledge through purposeful use of clarifying and guiding questions that help them organize their information and thinking, capture the essence of the new knowledge, and package that knowledge. Careful design of the learning experience ensures that learners can enjoy this collective discovery often.

Typically, learners want a quick fix, a recipe or a "how-to" that they can employ immediately. And why not? We all want recipes and easy answers when we can get them. Yet the most effective facilitation is to guide learners in an exploration of their own knowledge and experience. Thereby, learners build mental models (schemas) that serve them in future problem-solving situations. Although quick-fix recipes are sometimes useful, empowering learners to construct their own solutions strengthens their ability to understand the choices they make and enhances their self-confidence—the feeling that they *can* do whatever you're teaching them.

Capture Collective Capacities has three simple steps:

1. Pose a scenario that includes a question, problem, or challenge.
2. Elicit prior experience and knowledge.
3. Reveal distinctions that add insight or clarify their thinking.

Let's review each step in turn:

Pose a scenario: Introduce a challenging situation relevant to your topic. Set the scenario in a scene familiar to the learners: for educators perhaps a classroom or principal's council. In the business world, the setting may be an office, a meeting room, or hotel conference room. Describe characters, dialogue, and interactions to add emotional impact. It's helpful to have the scenario written out for each learner to see and reread if necessary. Here's a sample scenario for a workshop on facilitation:

A facilitator is standing at the front of a conference room, ready to begin a workshop. Participants sit at tables chatting among themselves. She begins the workshop with, "Good morning, everyone!" A few of the participants respond, but others continue talking. "Good morning, everyone!" the facilitator repeats, emphasizing the word everyone. The talking continues with a few glances toward her. The facilitator then asks participants to turn to page 10 in the workshop manual. Some follow her directions while others continue talking. What do you suggest she do?

Elicit prior experience and knowledge: After everyone has read the scenario, elicit what learners know or have done in similar situations. For example:

- How many of you know someone who has been in a similar situation?
- Have any of you experienced this situation?
- Is this behavior common? Under what circumstances or conditions is it most prevalent?
- Based on your experience, what do you do at the beginning of your workshop?

Reveal distinctions: Once everyone understands the situation and has shared what they know about or do in similar situations, continue to ask questions that lead to discernment and greater understanding. Choose questions that clarify participants' thinking and perhaps that explore additional options. By asking additional questions, you support, strengthen, or challenge what they know and do. Examples of the types of questions you might ask are

- What is your desired outcome for the first few minutes of your workshop?
- During the opening moments of your workshop, what messages do you want to send about learning and participating?
- How does what your learners do support the outcome?
- How could you open your workshop in a different way that would strengthen your desired outcome?

Making It Mine

Take a moment and write out a scenario you could use in your next workshop.

1. Consider the participants' real-life work situations (or students' learning requirements) as you create a scenario that captures their attention. You know you've got a good scenario when the participants begin to nod their heads or verbalize their recognition and acknowledgment.
2. Next list questions that elicit their prior knowledge and experience.
3. Finally, visualize your next class or workshop and choose a moment when Capture Collective Capacities would be appropriate. Hear yourself reading the scenario aloud as the participants read to themselves. Hear yourself asking your initial questions and imagine how they would respond.
4. Now, based on these responses, list follow-up questions that reveal distinctions and clarify or expand their thinking.

Oh, one more tip: Context is everything! You can create an atmosphere where Capture Collective Capacities is maximized and participants' intellectual capital is honored by implementing three guiding principles. When participants state and acknowledge these principles, they set the context for facilitation of knowledge to flourish. The three principles?

- Honor yourself by being self-directed: Take the initiative for your learning. Your thoughts matter.
- Honor others by being collectively managed.
- Act with a heightened sense of responsibility and respect toward others.

Invite your learners to co-create an atmosphere that fosters and maintains these three principles. How do we establish such an atmosphere? We have found it very desirable to offer adult learners a menu of possible scenarios to ensure success. We might present the principles and invite participants to practice them metacognitively (that is, thinking about what they do as they do it). We might then challenge them periodically by asking how we can work together more effectively. Or we might present a real-life metaphor of how these principles were effective and successful in a situation similar to the one participants are presently in.

Thinking It Over

What has been the greatest benefit of using Capture Collective Capacities?

_____

_____

_____

_____

_____

_____

_____

What results have I seen?

_____

_____

_____

_____

_____

_____

_____

What would I do differently next time?

_____

_____

_____

_____

_____

_____

_____

_____

Believing that learners know more than they think they do empowers them to build on their prior knowledge, clarify their choices, and expand their options.

HotTips for Facilitators ©2003 Zephyr Press • www.zephyrpress.com

Remind,
Don't Rescue

Promote initiative and problem solving
using this strategy.

In our desire to help, we are tempted to move too soon, speak
too quickly. Our intention is good. We want to ensure that our
participants succeed, and we are ready and eager to help. But
sometimes our desire to help actually impedes their ability to think.
In fact, we may snatch their brains from the jaws of great learning.
What can we do about it? Remind rather than rescue; question
rather than answer. Here's a suggestion.

After you've taught a lesson or provided the necessary information
for the next activity and participants begin their task, step back.
Refrain from responding for a moment. Refrain from calming the
waters or rushing to intervene. Give them a moment to get started
and settle in to the activity. Because people have been conditioned
to receive immediate assistance, there may be a hand or two
requesting your help. Or you may see one of the groups struggling
to get started or to cooperate with one another. Acknowledge that
you'll be there in a moment, give a nonverbal signal that
communicates "wait," and suggest they take a moment to figure
it out. It's in the moment of trying to figure out a problem that
thinking gets good! Jean Piaget and other cognitive development
experts since him remind us that learning takes place when new
information, ideas, or concepts challenge what we thought we

knew (see, for example, Scholnick et al. 1999). The disequilibrium created when we attempt to make sense of the new idea in relation to our current thinking is called cognitive dissonance. By allowing learners time to figure out a problem on their own, we allow cognitive dissonance to occur, thereby building their capacity to learn, think, and problem-solve.

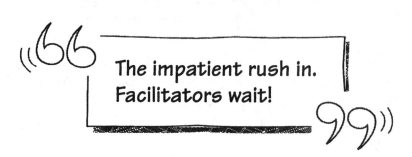

The impatient rush in. Facilitators wait!

After a few moments, walk around and check in. If participants need your help, ask questions that guide them to a solution. Remind them of what they know and the skills they possess that could help them solve the problem, answer the question, or work more cooperatively. Remember to ask clarifying questions that stimulate their thinking. For example:

- Where are you now?
- What are you trying to accomplish?
- Where are you stuck or what do you need to know?
- Where could you find the answer you are looking for?
- How would you know that you had the best answer?

Remember: You inspire, they perspire! Whether your participants are children or adults, your goal is to create more competent thinkers and problem solvers. If you always solve their problems, you create mere machines doing a task by rote instead of thinking it through. By allowing participants time to develop understanding and prompting their thinking using questions, you give them what they need to become better thinkers.

Making It Mine

Replay a lesson or training in your mind, focusing on a segment where the participants worked independently or in small groups. Analyze how well you allowed cognitive dissonance to occur. Watch what you did and listen to what you said. What enhancements would you make next time to really challenge the participants to think?

_____

_____

_____

_____

_____

_____

_____

_____

The next time you stand at the front of the room, put on your Remind, Don't Rescue personality. Inform participants that for the next three hours (or whatever time period) it's all about them, and all answers will arise from them. This communicates your expectations and creates a sense of participant responsibility by inviting them to join a process where your role is that of "the asker of questions"—prompting questions, provocative questions, challenging questions. Inform them that for the next three hours you have no answers, only questions.

Doing this may be challenging for you as a facilitator, and will be fun, interesting, and full of value for you and your participants. Be brave, gather all of your Fingertip Questions (see page 44), and enjoy the ride!

Thinking It Over

What worked well? How do I know I was successful?

_____

_____

_____

_____

_____

_____

When I remind rather than rescue I am reminded that participants . . .

_____

_____

_____

_____

What differences have I seen in my facilitation and participants' responses since I have been using this technique?

_____

_____

_____

_____

> Each time I wait or ask clarifying questions, my participants become better thinkers. The less I rescue, the more they think.

HotTips for Facilitators ©2003 Zephyr Press • www.zephyrpress.com

That Was Then, This Is Now

Set your expectations for participation.

Participants come to us with a mindset about how workshops, classes, learning, teaching, or school operate, based on their previous experiences. They have adopted a set of expectations that "this is the way things are supposed to be." This mindset often may hinder their involvement ("That's not the way Mr. B. did it." "In the other training we didn't have to do that."), impede their participation in activities ("I'll kick back and see if I can get away with taking the path of least resistance."), and interfere with their learning and thinking.

A simple conversation about how learning happens and participants' need to take ownership of it will help them make a smoother transition into the learning situation you are facilitating. Here's an example from a school setting:

"When you were younger, less mature, or in another class, things were different. You may not have been required to think at the levels you'll be challenged with in here. You may have been able to kick back and still get by, slip through, go unnoticed. That was then.

"Now you are older and more able to handle challenges. Here you'll learn and think in ways that perhaps you've always wanted to. You'll be monitoring your own progress, acquiring skills and knowledge that let you show your true abilities. This is now: a new place, a new time, and a new kind of learning experience for you. It may be challenging and at times uncomfortable, yet I know you have what it takes."

In a meeting situation, this HotTip may sound like this:

"Until this point we've allowed ourselves the luxury of tossing around ideas, making suggestions, and providing options. And we've done so without the constraints of implementation protocols. The brainstorming stage excites and invigorates us with the passion of our business.

"Beginning now we focus our energies on the best solutions and their efficient implementation. This stage, although equally invigorating, requires a different level of participation; a different level of thinking. Now is when the work begins. It's easy to brainstorm possibilities. It's more challenging to translate those possibilities into action. As we continue, consider each of your areas of influence. Speak from the point of view of your department while holding on to the goal we have set. Doing so provides the vantage points necessary to move our ideas into action."

Like deliberately pushing the reset button on your computer, this simple but powerful reminder puts participants' experience in perspective. It resets the context for them. It defines the quality and level of participation required for them to maximize their learning.

Making It Mine

Take a moment and write your responses to
the following questions, in order to craft your
own That Was Then, This Is Now talk.

In terms of attitude, behavior, quality of work,
quality of communication, and relationships,
what expectations do I have for participants?

_____

_____

_____

_____

What specifically will they be required to do (write, speak, think,
listen, and so on)?

_____

_____

_____

_____

I believe they can do it. I believe they have what it takes to meet or
exceed my expectations. What would telling them so sound like?

_____

_____

_____

_____

Based on things participants have said or done, what can I say
about their previous experiences? How can I seek to understand
their experiences?

_____

_____

_____

_____

What are participants' mindsets about learning, their school or work environment, classmates/colleagues, teachers/supervisors, and so on?

_____

_____

_____

_____

_____

_____

Now take a moment to outline a version of That Was Then, This Is Now appropriate for your class or workshop. Remember to describe specific behaviors and attitudes generic to most participants in your situation. Providing specifics helps them more easily understand your expectations. Addressing common, generic topics (attitude, talking, disorganization, hastiness, and the like) ensures that no one feels singled out. You can use the sentence starters provided or feel free to create your own.

"That Was Then" Sentence Starters

- You may be used to . . .
- In the past you may have been able to . . .
- Up until now you may have thought . . .
- Some of you may have been thinking that this is just like . . .

"This Is Now" Sentence Starters

- Something you may not know that will help you tremendously is . . .
- You'll have the opportunity to . . .
- You'll be glad to know that . . .
- Imagine when you'll be able to . . .

Thinking It Over

What worked well when I implemented this
HotTip? How do I know it was successful?

_____
_____
_____
_____
_____

What will I do differently next time to make this strategy more
effective?

_____
_____
_____
_____

When I use That Was Then, This Is Now, I am reminded that
participants . . .

_____
_____
_____
_____
_____

> By using That Was Then, This Is
> Now, I help participants shift their
> perspective about their experience
> as learners.

Anticipate the Next Move

Use a set of mental questions to help identify when you need to alter your agenda.

A prevalent saying among those in facilitation is, "The map is not the territory." Although we may have mapped out the road through our lesson or workshop, the actual terrain may be full of surprises! Some of our best lessons and agendas look great on paper . . . and then the participants arrive. When they do, the dynamics change; although the outcome may still be the same, the route may have to be altered slightly. This is what makes facilitation so exciting. It's the human dynamic that makes the predictable unpredictable. Anticipate the Next Move can help us navigate smoothly when we have to make slight or even massive alterations to our plans. Simply put, Anticipate the Next Move is a set of mental questions that can keep us just ahead of the ever-changing dynamics of a learning situation. It works like this: While participants are engaged in an activity, pause for a moment and ask yourself any or all of the following questions:

- What might happen next?
- What needs to happen next?
- What guidance or prompting do they need?
- What question would be best for them to consider at this point?
- What can they do to strengthen what they have just learned?

- How will I recognize when they are wrapping up the present task?
- Based on what I'm seeing, hearing, and feeling, where is this process (discussion, group work) going? Is it still on track toward the outcome, or are we wandering astray?

After considering these questions and making observations, plan subsequent tasks accordingly.

Making It Mine

In our personal lives we often Anticipate the Next Move. Whether we're driving, doing a chore, cooking, or conversing with family and friends, we naturally seek patterns and make predictions. This ability allows us to stay focused and engaged. For the next 24 hours, be aware of instances when you Anticipate the Next Move. Notice when you act on your predictions and when you wait to gather more information.

Now apply this to your professional life. Consider a lesson you've taught or a workshop you've led recently. Review in your mind a time when the participants were discussing, brainstorming, analyzing, or the like. As you recall their conversation or responses, practice asking yourself the preceding questions. Remember this is just a practice exercise, so feel free to stop the mental video, rewind, and choose a different question. Consider how you would answer each question and how the process might be altered based on your answers.

While you're in the practice mode, let's do one more application of this HotTip in a scenario:

You are asked to facilitate a group where you know you will be faced with tremendous resistance. Participants do not want to be there, and you have three hours to spend with them. You are already anticipating their thoughts and feelings and are concerned with how you might react to what they might ask or say.

In your best facilitator mode, anticipate your response to the following statements. There are alternative endings to several of the statements. Choose the version that best fits your setting (or make up your own). Write out what you would say. This exercise will undoubtedly increase your Rolodex of responses!

"We really don't want to be here. It has nothing to do with you, of course."

_____

_____

_____

"This is the same old stuff. Not again!"

_____

_____

_____

"This won't work with my kids/in my work setting."

_____

_____

_____

"Why are we learning this? It has nothing to do with my job requirements/my school/my class."

_____

_____

_____

"You'd better be good or we're out of here at break."

_____

_____

_____

"We're only here because we're getting paid for it/we have no choice."

_____

_____

_____

Thinking It Over

What value did you gain from implementing Anticipate the Next Move?

_____

_____

_____

_____

_____

_____

How did this technique propel your participants' learning?

_____

_____

_____

_____

_____

Anticipating the Next Move allows me to stay resourceful and flexible.

Ride the Winds
of Fate

Use this strategy to heighten participants'
curiosity, creativity, and attentiveness.

There's nothing like a good challenge to pique curiosity, stimulate new thinking, or redirect focus and attention. Riding the Winds of Fate is the purposeful introduction of a "change of plans." Whereas the next tip, Call an Audible, is spontaneous and based on the events of the moment, the use of this HotTip is predetermined, although it appears spontaneous to the participants. It involves the insertion of new directions, questions, or criteria not stated in the opening directions for an activity. Presenting something you intended to do as an "unpredictable event" increases the challenge, pace, quality, or meaning of the experience. For example, decreasing the time allowed to complete an activity or announcing that groups will have to make presentations to their peers increases participants' level of concern, thereby heightening their attention and motivation to produce. Here are a few suggestions:

- Decrease the amount of time available to solve a problem or challenge. Request that the same amount of work be accomplished in half the time, for example.

- With a written assignment, announce that participants have to make an oral presentation as well. In a workshop, each participant might present his or her work to the whole group or share within a small group. Students might make a presentation to their own class, another class, the principal, or a community organization (such as Kiwanis, Rotary, YMCA).

- If participants are working in groups, request that they be silent for the rest of the time, communicating using gestures or sign language.
- In a project, raise your expectations for quality through requiring use of more resources, key vocabulary words, better penmanship, clearer graphics, proper grammar, more precise descriptions, and the like. Then check to ensure the quality is produced.
- Turn an independent project or assignment into a partner project, or vice versa.

Making It Mine

Think of an upcoming activity for your participants, perhaps a project, flow chart, implementation design, game, worksheet, reading assignment, or lab write-up. What is one direction you could introduce during the activity that would increase the demand for quantity, quality, effort, creativity, collaborative work, or independent work?

If you are interested in raising participants' level of concern about a presentation, require that the presentation be done with pizzazz and include an interactive activity. Instead of cutting the time for an activity, allow them extra time to enhance their presentation. Granting extra time employs a bit of reverse psychology. Participants' level of concern is heightened not because of a shortage of time, but rather because they feel obliged to use the extra time to do the best job possible. Here are a few simple suggestions for additional directions you might introduce:

- Each group member must be involved in the design and delivery of the presentation.

- Incorporate interactive strategies for listener involvement in your presentation.
- Be sure to use a variety of media.
- Implement effective presentation and facilitation techniques.
- Create a powerful opening and closing to your presentation.
- Include aspects that appeal to various learning styles (such as visual, auditory, and kinesthetic) or intelligences (such as interpersonal, bodily-kinesthetic, and musical-rhythmic).
- Choose the type of feedback you would like to receive about your presentation.

Thinking It Over

What benefits have I seen since I've begun Riding the Winds of Fate?

_____

_____

_____

_____

_____

_____

_____

_____

When I Ride the Winds of Fate, I am reminded that my participants . . .

_____

_____

_____

_____

_____

_____

_____

_____

What would I do differently next time I use this HotTip?

_____

_____

_____

_____

_____

_____

_____

_____

> **Each time I Ride the Winds of Fate, I add novelty to the learning experience and increase motivation.**

Call an Audible

Use this strategy for changing your plan for a lesson or workshop when something unexpected happens.

Imagine that you are in the middle of a well-designed lesson or training session. You've asked participants to gather in small groups and discuss solutions to a critical problem you presented. About halfway through the allotted time, you observe that the initial topic has given way to a parallel issue and that everyone is engaged in the conversation.

You wonder what happened. Did you not clearly define the context for this conversation? You quickly review what you said and decide that the setup was fine. What do you do? Call an Audible! You've already made your own assessment of the situation by listening to the conversations and watching participants' body language. Now verify your assessment and, based on participants' feedback, decide whether to redirect them to the original plan or to modify the plan.

In the preceding discussion example, you might ask everyone to find a place to pause and then say something like, "As I've tuned in to your conversations, it seems that you've found value in talking about a different issue. Who would be willing to clarify this new issue?" Hands go up and one participant begins to share the highlights of her group's conversation so far. Another participant suggests that this new issue is actually an essential component of the initial issue. Now, you make the call. "How about if we continue with this new issue for the next 15 minutes and move the discussion toward three viable solutions?" Everyone agrees and they're off!

When Calling an Audible keep in mind these three steps:

1. **Assess the situation:** Walk around and gather data regarding participants' understanding of the original assignment and where they might be getting stuck or sidetracked. Watch, listen, and feel. Look for physical cues of engagement and interest. Listen to the conversations. Ask yourself, "What am I hearing, seeing, and sensing? Is everyone moving forward with the discussion or activity?"

2. **Verify your assessment with the group or class:** If you observe that things are not going as you had expected, check to see if your observations and perceptions are accurate. For example, "It seems to me that the issue arising from your conversation is _____. Is that true?" or "It looks to me as if you've figured out how to solve these equations and can do them accurately. Raise your hand if you agree."

3. **Make the call:** Suggest a different tack or a change of plans based on your assessment and the group's feedback. For example, "May I suggest, then, that we alter our course slightly and work toward a solution to this issue?" Or "How about if everyone solves one more problem, giving it your best thinking. Based on how you do, we'll discuss what your homework might be." Often it is useful to explain how the altered course still fits into the overall outcome of the workshop or lesson.

In our experience with facilitation, how well Calling an Audible works is directly related to the level of rapport we have with the group and our ability to relate the change of direction to the desired outcome of the activity or lesson. This is a skill you will refine with practice, and the first time you Call an Audible is often the most precarious. With practice, however, you'll be calling audibles with precision.

Making It Mine

When, during the course of a normal day, do you naturally Call an Audible? Play back the last 24 hours and allow those moments to bubble up in your mind. Under what circumstances are you most likely to Call an Audible? What is the setting? Are you with others? Alone? Are you teaching, facilitating, or presenting? What impels you to Call an Audible?

Now imagine that you are facilitating a group that is sharp and fast-paced. You realize that traditional activities are too easy and will bore this group. They need some punch to their activity, a challenge in their process. Read the following scenarios. Then, Call an Audible and replace the traditional activity with a new, full-of-punch challenge.

Scenario 1: You are giving a 20-minute mini-lecture on effective facilitation. Instead you Call an Audible and . . .

_____

_____

_____

Scenario 2: You had planned for everyone to read an article and then discuss it in small groups. Instead you Call an Audible and . . .

_____

_____

_____

Scenario 3: You have 15 minutes left in your lesson or workshop. You wonder whether this would be a good time to present one more chunk of information. Instead you Call an Audible and . . .

_____

_____

_____

HotTips for Facilitators ©2003 Zephyr Press • www.zephyrpress.com

Thinking It Over

What observations would lead you to Call an Audible?

_____

_____

_____

_____

_____

_____

_____

What would you need to see or hear to be certain that Calling an Audible is the best choice?

_____

_____

_____

_____

_____

_____

_____

> When I Call an Audible, I validate and respect the concerns of my participants.

Plan Fingertip Questions

Preplan or spontaneously use practical, adaptable, probing questions.

Since the time of Socrates the value of good questions has gone undisputed. Because effective facilitators believe that participants know more than they think they do, we are always in search of the right question at the right time. Questions cause us to seek answers, interpret, predict, ponder, discover, and make meaning. The skillful use of questions can elegantly guide participants to powerful results.

Here are a host of questions that we have used or that have been used on us. They have a wide variety of uses and can be modified to fit nearly any situation. We call them Fingertip Questions because they're handy to have at our fingertips:

- What are your outcomes?
- What will success look, sound, and feel like?
- What are your consistent challenges?
- What performance measures will indicate you have met your goal?
- What is it you see me doing?
- How are you navigating this process?
- What's working?

- What has yet to work?
- How could we change to produce different results?
- What needs to be in place for our desired outcome to happen?
- What's important for us to know or do in order to move forward?
- What new mechanisms need to be in place to ensure we move forward?
- How do we get to the next level of clarity?
- What are the necessary conditions for this meeting to be effective?
- What is positive about your problem?
- What is not perfect yet?
- What are we willing to do to make this situation the way we want it to be?
- What are we willing to no longer do in order to make this situation the way we want it?
- Does _____ meet your needs?
- Does _____ build capacity?
- Is _____ sustainable?
- How are you going to measure your return on investment?
- How can we capture the successes, solutions, and challenges from those who have stories?
- How do we make this plan work?
- What are we doing to counter the challenges?
- What was your outcome?
- As a result of your outcome, what will be different in the larger system?
- What would your supporters say to you?
- What would your critics say?
- What advice might a mentor give to you?
- What would you change?

- What is the purpose of our work?
- Are we clear now?
- Where do we go from here?
- What have been the highlights so far?
- Why won't this plan work?
- Where are the landmines?
- How well is our work pattern geared to the needs of our customers?
- Why is our work done the way it is?
- How flexible are we?
- How prepared are we for the unexpected?
- What kind of school/organization/department/team do we want to become?
- If we had complete freedom, how would we organize our work?
- How would we like our work to be?
- How could our work be done differently?
- What do you believe would improve it?

The following questions are for the brave. They are superb questions to ask yourself or pose to your workshop participants:

- What is my life calling me to do?
- How can I raise the stakes?
- How good am I willing to let my life get?
- If I look back over my life, what is my place in the world?
- What is expressed to the world through me?
- What is my life work?
- If I knew I couldn't fail, what would I do?
- What do I have the courage to be in life?

Making It Mine

Which questions caught your attention?
Read through the list again. Which questions do you hear yourself asking? Record
your top five below.

1. _____
2. _____
3. _____
4. _____
5. _____

Thinking It Over

What is the connection between the quality
of the question we ask and the quality of the
answer we get?

_____
_____
_____
_____
_____
_____

Think about the last facilitation you did. Where did you ask the
right question at the right time? What was the result?

Question: _____

_____
_____

Result: _____

_____
_____

When else during the event could you have asked a question?
What would likely have been the result if you had?

Question opportunity: _____

_____

_____

Likely result: _____

_____

_____

> Having questions at my fingertips moves my participants toward powerful results and equips me for the unexpected.

Pause, Be Silent, and Attend

Take opportunities to create long-lasting impact.

▶ **When is being silent exactly the right thing to do?**

▶ **Where will I pause to foster and direct maximum participant attentiveness?**

These are two questions to explore during the course of any facilitation. Effective facilitators practice the purposeful use of silence and pauses as two powerful tools to heighten the participants' attentiveness to a significant learning moment. There are many creative possibilities to pique interest through silence and pauses: to add punch to a statement, to offer a moment for reflection, to redirect attention and move to the next thought, or simply to add "edutainment" value to the moment. We highly recommend you design silence and pauses into your events, even though opportunities will unfold for you to implement the strategy spontaneously. So, don't simply be ready to use silence, be *sure* to use it. By modeling this behavior, you also will encourage your participants to do the same.

Given that we deeply value our participants' contributions, we use Pause, Be Silent, and Attend to validate what they have to say. Explore and experiment with the following strategies to increase impact, respect, and personal reflection.

Making It Mine

First, what strategies do you use now to ensure that participants' comments are respected and given time to be reflected upon?

_____

_____

_____

_____

_____

_____

_____

_____

During your next facilitation, after a participant shares a comment, question, thought, or idea, model yourself as a listening, compassionate facilitator by

- pausing to look in the direction from which the question came
- standing silent and fairly still
- reflecting on what was said and how it furthers the desired outcome of your event
- allowing five to seven seconds of silence before responding or moving to the next participant

Participants notice when you listen and think about their comments or questions. Most will get the message that you feel each contribution is important, value reflection, and honor participants for sharing. If after all your exemplary modeling participants still aren't catching on, bring your behavior to their attention. Invite them to experiment with silence and reflection by pausing five to seven seconds after a comment has been made.

Thinking It Over

How has using this strategy influenced the
level of participation?

_____

_____

_____

_____

_____

How has Pause, Be Silent, and Attend changed what I do as a
facilitator?

_____

_____

_____

_____

How has Pause, Be Silent, and Attend changed the emotional tone
of my trainings or lessons?

_____

_____

_____

_____

> I honor participants' contribu-
> tions each time I employ Pause,
> Be Silent, and Attend.

Every Body
Tells a Story

Use physical cues to deduce participants' emotions or mood.

As facilitators, we manage multiple dynamics simultaneously
during the course of any learning event. We think about the
content, questions to ask, levels of interaction, comfort, noise level,
when to break, and possible next steps. This HotTip invites you to
increase your awareness of nonverbal group and human dynamics.
Nonverbal communication powerfully affects the flow and value
of a learning event. Challenge your sensory acuity by practicing a
careful and purposeful "visual read" of what people say with their
bodies.

Have you ever heard of BMIRS? (bee´ mers, *n*)? We originally heard
this acronym from Suzanne Bailey, of Bailey and Associates, during
a workshop on facilitation skills. BMIRS stands for Behavioral
Manifestations of Internal Response Systems. Said differently, what
we feel and think on the inside will show up on the outside. Our
feelings, emotions, and thoughts manifest themselves through
some part of our body. Unlike words, the body rarely lies. As
responsive facilitators, it is prudent to be acutely aware of the
external cues our participants offer us.

We realize this is not an exact science. But even though there may
be multiple possible interpretations of the same behavioral manifestations, the greater our sensitivity to participants' physical cues,
the more in tune we can be to their internal learning processes.

Making It Mine

The ability to notice and interpret BMIRS as they unfold is learned. The following are some easily noticed behavioral manifestations. Use the list to practice your sensory acuity. We invite you to use all your acumen to guess as many reasons as possible why a participant might display each item on the list. This is not a right or wrong exercise. It is more an exercise in interpretation that reminds us not to pigeonhole a behavioral manifestation as having a specific meaning. For example, we might cross our arms because we feel defensive or simply because we feel cold. To make this HotTip yours, write on the line next to each behavioral manifestation what the participant might be thinking or feeling on the inside. Ask yourself, "What internal responses would cause the participant to reveal these BMIRS?"

Behavioral Manifestation	Possible Internal Responses
Flared nostrils	_____
Blinking	_____
Leaning forward	_____
Change of face color	_____
Rapid breathing	_____
Eye contact	_____
Large hand gestures	_____
Bent posture	_____
Smiling expression	_____
No expression	_____
Rapid movements	_____
Moist hands	_____
Closed fist	_____
Crossed arms	_____
Higher than usual vocal pitch	_____
Rapid speech	_____

Now, if you wish, see our ideas on page 122.

Thinking It Over

Which of these manifestations have very predictable internal responses?

_____

_____

_____

Which ones are relatively hard to interpret?

_____

_____

_____

Which BMIRS do I see most often?

_____

_____

_____

What have been the major benefits of enhancing my perceptiveness?

_____

_____

_____

Recognizing BMIRS increases my ability to foster rapport.

Know Their Hearts

Unlock the door to your participants' hearts.

Daniel Goleman, in his brilliant book *Emotional Intelligence* (1995), theorizes that deep within each of us is an emotional intelligence that is superordinate over our intellect. Some believe emotional intelligence actually guides and orchestrates the other intelligences. This concept has radically changed how we facilitate. We used to believe that to reach our participants emotionally, we first would have to reach them intellectually. Now, in contrast, we believe that to reach participants at all, we first must touch their hearts.

As facilitators, we have opportunities to deepen the impact of our work not only by engaging the emotional intelligence of our participants, but also by engaging, enriching, and deepening our own emotional intelligence. This HotTip invites you to explore your personal emotional quotient through self-reflection as well as to learn strategies that facilitate participant reflectiveness. Here is our condensed version of emotional intelligence (affectionately known as E.I.). There are five dimensions of E.I.:

Self-knowledge: being aware of your own emotions

Self-control: controlling your own emotions

Empathy: noticing and recognizing the emotions of others

Social skills: building relationships and facilitating interaction

Self-motivation: being able to motivate yourself

As you scan this list, do you notice a commonality or recurring theme? The word *self* is embedded in nearly every dimension of this intelligence. Thus, to be effective and constantly improve as facilitators, we must begin with ourselves. The questions, "Who am I as a facilitator?" and "In what ways are my actions a reflection of my beliefs and attitudes?" get to the heart of emotional intelligence. One of our mentors once told us, "You can only take a group where you yourselves have gone." In the context of E.I., we can only reach a group's heart to the depth we have reached into our own. Taking time for self-reflection and connecting with our inner selves sets a solid foundation so that we can stay the steady course of an event and facilitate elegantly in the moment. Knowing, understanding, and managing our inner thoughts and emotions are of paramount importance. The more appropriately our internal worlds are managed, the more present we can be to facilitate the process and interactions of an event.

To be effective facilitators, we need to be aware of our inner thoughts and emotions while guiding the event. We must constantly be reading the participants' verbal and nonverbal emotional cues. And finally, facilitation is all about relationships, about our ability to lead and direct others to a desired outcome.

Here are ideas for amplifying the five dimensions of E.I. to engage and enrich yourself and your participants:

Self-knowledge: Offer your participants opportunities to practice metacognition, understanding inner conflicts, and recognizing and differentiating their own emotions. Remind them often to think about their own thinking (metacognition). We often ask our participants to think about their own thinking as they engage in activities that incorporate the multiple intelligences. They listen to their inner voices to recognize how they feel about doing the various intelligence-tapping activities. They listen to their own thinking and learn.

Self-control: First, be in control of your own emotions. For you and your participants alike, this means refining your ability to control impulsiveness, delay gratification, and interrupt the escalation of emotions.

Empathy: Empathy means learning to stand in another's shoes, think their thoughts, and take on their roles. Strategies that will engage us include interpreting nonverbal clues as well as recognizing and discriminating others' emotions.

Social skills: Model active and successful leadership toward an objective or goal. Display genuine friendship and effective listening. A key component of the social skills dimension is the ability to manage conflict whenever it should arise.

Self-motivation: Both you and your participants can begin by setting realistic and attainable goals for the event or workshop. You can do this by analyzing your tasks and processes into doable components. By managing time effectively, you stay in control of the event and have the confidence to attain your goals for it.

Making It Mine

Take a day (like tomorrow) and heighten your awareness of E.I.'s five dimensions. Perhaps choose one dimension at a time to focus on for an hour. Look, listen, and feel for characteristics that put you in touch with your own and others' emotional intelligence.

During your next facilitation, increase your awareness of your participants' emotional intelligence. Remember to use empathetic traits such as care, compassion, forgiveness, understanding, patience, kindness, humor, and appreciation. They will serve you well and promote an atmosphere of mutual respect and appreciation at your event. Choose a dimension and think of at least two strategies that would enhance it.

Dimension: _____

_____

Strategies:

1. _____

2. _____

Thinking It Over

At what point do my participants get "plugged in" emotionally? What do I do when that happens?

_____

_____

_____

_____

_____

_____

What did I do today to enhance the emotional intelligence of people around me?

_____

_____

_____

_____

_____

What can I do tomorrow to enrich my own emotional intelligence?

_____

_____

_____

_____

_____

> When I remember to Know Their Hearts, I remember to know my own as well.

Celebrate Resistance

Honor, acknowledge, and dance with the
energy present in the group.

We were asked to facilitate a three-day event, "The Art and Magic of Effective Presentations." On entering the room, we immediately noticed resistance in the audience. Participants' arms were crossed and their body language clearly stated that they did not want to be there. By one minute into our opening, we were certain of participants' resistance through their skeptical looks, inattentive behavior, and complete non-cooperation. What did we do, you ask? We did the unexpected: we "un-resisted." Instead of becoming annoyed at their lack of participation and pushing forward with increased enthusiasm (as if ignoring their behavior and attitude would make them go away), we asked for feedback about our opening. At that point, the group presented us with straightforward and blunt information: They said we had started 30 minutes late! No wonder they were less than receptive! After we acknowledged their annoyance and apologized for the miscommunication about the start time, we had a very successful day.

There is a universal law of nature to which we facilitators must adhere: Fighting resistance only makes resistance stronger. For example, imagine that a participant voices a complaint. If we meet the complaint with inquisition, logic, or self-justification, we resist resistance, thereby feeding it even more. "It takes two to tango" applies here. Resistance can exist only when we resist it. As effective facilitators we must learn to dissipate resistance by celebrating it. By listening closely and paraphrasing to verify our understanding, we help to drain away resistance and establish high levels of respect and rapport. We invite you to explore a few of our favorite strategies for Celebrating Resistance.

Anticipate and Address Resistance

Anticipate possible reasons for resistance and incorporate them into your presentation. Should resistance surface, participants will assume it is part of the presentation. It will seem not to be resistance at all. To use this strategy effectively, we use artfully vague language, letting each participant tailor his or her own understanding of our meaning.

Sometimes resistance stems from participants' feelings of either inferiority or superiority. We've experienced both dynamics: situations where we have been younger and less experienced than the group we are facilitating and others where our reputation has been blown out of proportion and the audience has unrealistic expectations. We offer you a strategy that places you as the facilitator in a "one-down" position, a position on the same footing as or one step down from the participants. The result is to shift the focus from your expertise to the participants' expertise and to eliminate the potential for power struggles. The following script is one way to accomplish this strategy. Feel free to use it as is, or challenge yourself to rewrite and reword it to fit your personal style:

"I don't pretend to be a better facilitator than you or any other facilitator. My work has led me to understand the multiple dynamics of presenting and facilitating to achieve maximum results, and I have learned many strategies and different ways to facilitate learning environments. But I cannot begin to know the particular circumstances and situations in which you work. I, like you, am a learner doing the best I can at any given moment. Please bear with me if I offer some suggestions that don't fit your needs. Feel free to adopt those that will work for you and give me feedback about where I can strengthen my facilitative action and knowledge base."

It's All about Them

One of us experienced the ultimate in resistance when we were debriefing an experiential learning activity called "beyond boundaries." The participants (educational entrepreneurs from across the country) were in their fourth day of training. This activity was designed to push them just a bit further in their thinking, stretch their comfort zones one more time, and lead them to consider options outside their current realm of understanding. Although the activity is a fast-paced, laughter-rich, complex experience, the debriefing segment is deep, meaningful, and poignant.

In the middle of the debriefing, Ian, a young man in his thirties, bolted to his feet and loudly proclaimed, "This is a @#&!-ing waste of my time! I can't believe I've paid all this money to be jerked through some silly activity that has no apparent meaning. You don't know what you are talking about, and I've had it." The audience was stunned to silence. No one moved. All eyes were on Ian, including mine. You can imagine how I felt standing in front of 150 people, most of whom were older than I was. As I struggled to keep breathing and maintain my composure, I luckily remembered the facilitator's axiom, "It's all about them . . . always." I took a step closer to him. He began venting again. I kept breathing, holding eye contact, and maintaining a calm exterior. When he paused to catch his breath, I took another step closer and said, "Thank you." Ian looked at me with confusion. This was the magical moment. I didn't resist his resistance. I welcomed it with the intent to understand it, not defend myself. After a little more dialogue and respect for his feelings, Ian calmed down and the other participants began coming both to his and my aid. The facilitation gods were with me during that moment, and out of it has come a relentless commitment to meet resistance with grace and celebration. Remember: It's all about them, so seek to understand their perspective and stay connected.

Making It Mine

Recall an event in the past week when you encountered resistance. Play it over in your mind so that you are clear about the order of events and the dialogue. Did you resist or Celebrate Resistance? If you resisted, how would you respond differently next time? If you Celebrated Resistance, think about how you did so and the qualities you exhibited during the event.

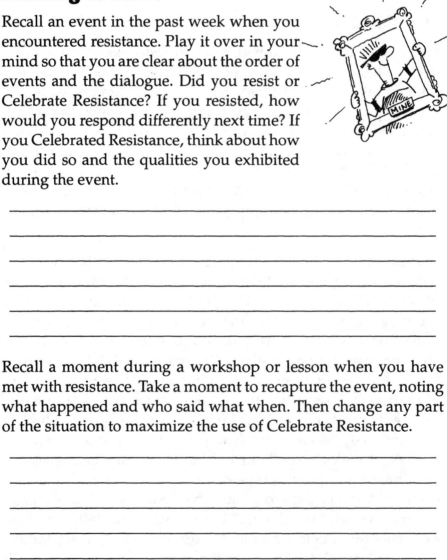

_____

_____

_____

_____

_____

_____

Recall a moment during a workshop or lesson when you have met with resistance. Take a moment to recapture the event, noting what happened and who said what when. Then change any part of the situation to maximize the use of Celebrate Resistance.

_____

_____

_____

_____

_____

_____

Thinking It Over

On a scale of 1 to 10, where 1 is "not even close" and 10 is "It's a party!" where am I with Celebrating Resistance? _____

What could I do to increase my ability to Celebrate Resistance?

_____

_____

_____

_____

_____

_____

_____

_____

" Every time I Celebrate Resistance, I open the doors to connection and rapport. "

Take Exits, On-Ramps, and Segues

Plan strategic transitions.

I magine that you are facilitating a group of leaders engaged in a lively dialogue. You know that if you let the conversation continue and collectively field comments, you will have to cut an important piece of content from your presentation because of time constraints. Have you ever been in that situation? Or imagine that you notice the audience checking out or discussing the same issue repeatedly. How do you move the group forward or to the next activity? Use the principle of Exits, On-Ramps, and Segues!

The language you use is critical because it's easy to give offense if you're not careful. We suggest simple transitional sentences that encourage groups to stop, put on hold, or redirect their conversations. Although what you say is important, how you say it and what you do while saying it often convey an even more powerful message.

Here are a few of our favorite phrases that provide an exit, an on-ramp to the next activity, or a smooth segue:

- "Let's stop the tape here."
- "May I pause this discussion here?"
- "Allow me to pause here."
- "I'd like to freeze what we're doing and put it on hold."
- "We are going to have to go offline."

- "Let's put a bookmark here."
- "Hang on, let's see where we should go next."
- "I'd like to step back from your question a bit and go a different way with it."

Making It Mine

First, what sentences do you use now to exit a conversation, merge to a new activity, or segue smoothly? List the top three phrases you currently use when facilitating.

1. _____

2. _____

3. _____

Before you tackle the following challenge, here's a quick tip. When you sense the need to make a transition, take a step back, breathe, and collect your thoughts. This physical and mental break from the moment allows you time to gain perspective and reorient yourself.

Here is the challenge: For each of the phrases we provided on pages 64–65, write one of your own. You can reword it to fit your style, or change just a word or two so that it conveys the same idea with a little refinement from you. Have fun!

_____

_____

_____

_____

_____

_____

_____

_____

_____

Thinking It Over

How are my transitions now compared to
before?

_____

_____

_____

_____

_____

_____

If I could give myself one piece of advice about transitions, what
would I say?

_____

_____

_____

_____

What benefit do my participants receive when my transitions are
smooth?

_____

_____

_____

_____

> Graceful yet purposeful Exits, On-
> Ramps, and Segues assist in
> navigating the group toward the
> desired outcomes.

Part 2
Activities and Processes

In teaching, training, and presenting, the content encompasses the information to be delivered (the what). In contrast, during facilitation the content is not what is to be delivered or solved, but rather lies in the how. How will participants reach a solution? Record their thinking? Explore possibilities? Organize their ideas? Implement what they've designed? Although these questions are considered and planned for in the design phase, the following HotTips ensure that these bases are covered.

This section begins with ways for participants to capture their thinking and explore any assumptions they may have about the topic to be learned or solved. In addition, there are tips to structure brainstorming sessions, prioritize ideas, and create implementation plans.

Create KnowBooks and Other Graphic Organizers

Use these graphic organizers to propel learning and recall.

Meaning-making is one of the things the brain does best (Caine and Caine 1994). Drawing on past experience and understanding, the brain searches for and creates meaning in every situation. We can capitalize on this innate talent by encouraging participants to create graphic organizers such as KnowBooks that propel their learning.

A KnowBook is a collection of notes, drawings, graphs, pictures, clippings, or the like that represent the knowledge a participant has accumulated. Think of it as a real-time portfolio of learning or a participant-created textbook or workshop notebook. It could take the form of a three-ring binder, an 8½" x 11" sketch book from an art supply store, a picture album, or even a stapled sheaf of papers. It has a cover page with an appropriate title (such as "Lynn's KnowBook") and a page for the table of contents (written when the KnowBook is completed). It is most effective for learners to do most of the writing and drawing themselves rather than simply cutting and pasting from other sources.

What might pages in the KnowBook contain?

- Handwritten notes (color-coded to assist memory) from a lecture or meeting, or information gleaned from a manual, textbook, or encyclopedia.
- Diagrams illustrating processes such as customer inquiries, the communication flow in your organization, the water cycle, how to solve a particular math problem, or the mechanisms of plate tectonics. Each diagram is labeled with pertinent information.
- Summaries or reflections about a given topic.
- Cartoons that diagram and summarize what the participant learned.
- Stories narrating "A Day in the Life of _____" (a Purchase Order, Memo, Beetle, Mathematical Variable, Amoeba, or whatever).

Other Possible Formats

One-Pagers and Interactive Notes are alternate formats that may be useful, particularly for relatively short-term applications. One-Pagers, originally developed by Gabriele Rico, invite learners to summarize their understanding in pictures and symbols, with or without words on a single page (see Rico n.d.; or visit Rico's website at www. gabrielerico.com).

Interactive Notes are preformatted note frames in which some but not all the information is provided. Key words, phrases, and illustrations are omitted, allowing participants to "fill-in-the-blanks" (see page 71). This format could be very effective for a workshop handout or meeting agenda. Be sure to provide space in the notes for participants to draw pictures, ask questions, or speculate.

Begin a mission to involve yourself and others in transforming one-dimensional handouts and manuals into multidimensional, interactive, intrapersonal avenues to engagement that accommodate different learning styles and preferred intelligences. Let your

(continued on page 73)

KnowBook Sample

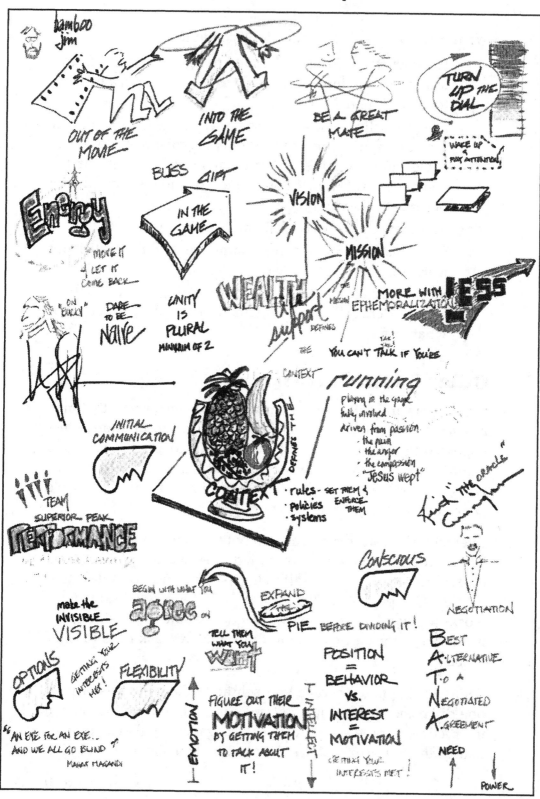

The Powerful Learning and Teaching Guide
Synthesizing what we know so we can do it efficiently!

Why a model?

1. Models _____ the complexity of our practice.
2. Models _____ our practice.
3. Models provide an _____ .
4. Common models:
   A) Promote _____ .
   B) Build _____ through _____ .
   C) Provide a system of _____ .

How did this model (guide) come to be?

- An attempt to answer: " _____
  _____
  _____
  _____ ?"

- A _____ of _____
  _____ and _____ .

How can I use this model (guide)?

1. To plan _____ and _____ .
2. To analyze _____ .
3. To compare _____ .
4. As a _____ .
5. As a way to _____ .

One-Pager Sample

participants' creative juices loose! As you can imagine, the possibilities are endless. And if you ever run out of ideas, simply ask participants to capture what they know about a given topic in their own way! Be prepared for amazing creativity!

Making It Mine

Your next training, meeting, unit of study, or lesson might be the perfect opportunity for participants to create their own KnowBook, One-Pager, or Interactive Notes. Ask yourself, "What would be the best form for this collection of knowledge? A bound book of blank pages? Blank sheets of paper? Some other medium?" Then ask, "In what ways could participants best represent this knowledge? Is it more effective for them to follow a prescribed format or create their own? How often will they record what they are learning?"

Here's a creative challenge for you. Take any existing lesson, handout, or trainer's manual your organization or school uses. Transform it into Interactive Notes. Ask yourself the following questions for each page you decide to transform.

- How can I increase the degree of participant interaction with this page?

- What can I change in the format that would cause them to write something down, fill something in, draw an image, ask a question, or think about an issue?

- How can I cause participants to interact with this page in such a manner that the information becomes richer and more meaningful for them?

Thinking It Over

Which of these graphic organizer formats do
my participants enjoy the most? Why?

_____

_____

_____

What improvements in learning have my participants demon-
strated since they've been using KnowBooks, One-Pagers, or
Interactive Notes?

_____

_____

_____

_____

Which type or types of graphic organizers seem to work best for
my needs and situation? How will I decide when to use graphic
organizers over traditional notes in the future?

_____

_____

_____

_____

Using KnowBooks, One-Pagers, or Interactive Notes allows participants to
make meaning for themselves and capture their new knowledge.

Take a Page

Use this reflective process to allow participants to unpack their internal dialogue and current mindsets in an environment that feels safe.

Have you ever walked into a meeting, workshop, seminar, or class with your mind made up about the value of the event before it even begins? Or sat through the opening moments of a presentation saying in your mind something like, "How is this really going to help me? I'm already pretty good at what I do. Is this really going to be worth my time?" Know that this internal dialogue is normal and healthy. It's our own way of making meaning and detecting purpose. This internal dialogue can either enhance our learning experience or greatly distract from it.

Peter Senge (1990) writes about the influence of assumptions on systemic thinking and on our ability to be agile learners. Participants arrive at our meetings, workshops, or classroom doors with a wide range of thoughts about the topic, the purpose of the learning experience, and the value they anticipate receiving from it. Allowing participants to express their expectations, concerns, and current mindsets establishes a common starting place while acknowledging the vast array of knowledge and experience each individual brings to the learning experience.

Take a Page is useful and powerful. The participants each take a sheet of paper and, guided by a set of questions, record their current thinking about the meeting, workshop, or course; its content; their expectations; and even their prior knowledge and experience. Page 77 shows a sample Take a Page a participant might receive during the opening of a daylong workshop for managers and business executives.

The questions could be written to glean the information you deem most appropriate for your meeting, workshop, or class. In addition, the "page" could be paper of any size, a white board, an index card, or other material. Choose the best medium for the topic of your event, the amount of room participants have to write, and the space available in the room. The important aspect of this activity is to guide people to reflect on and record their assumptions about the learning experience. They then can share their reflections aloud to the entire group (if the group is small), or in groups ranging from two or three to six or eight people. Each group could then give a summary of their reflections and what they want to get out of the learning experience so you can adapt your presentation to meet their needs. Secondary-level teachers or college instructors may choose to gather the papers for course planning. (Students need not sign their names.)

Making It Mine

Capture a time when you went to a workshop, meeting, or class. Recall the moments just prior to the event. What thoughts did you have about the day? What were you feeling and thinking as you anticipated the event? Jot a few of those on a piece of paper.

As you think about a workshop or class you facilitate, take a moment to enter the minds of your participants and see the event from their viewpoint. Capture what they might be thinking and feeling about the topic of the day. Now write a set of questions that would help participants record those thoughts and feelings. Ta-da! You've just created a Take a Page.

Take a Page

Everyone arrives at a workshop with a set of expectations about what they hope to accomplish or see fulfilled during their time. In addition, we all have our own viewpoints and assumptions about the challenge ahead. Taking the time to express our thoughts allows us to establish a common ground, clarify our thinking, and build mutual understanding.

Read the following list of questions. Then, using the paper provided, communicate your expectations and thoughts for today's focus. You have ten minutes of reflective time to record your thoughts, opinions, questions, feelings, and concerns. You may draw, Mind Map, list, cluster, write, create a poem or song, or use any other method that feels comfortable for you. Be prepared to share your "page" with others.

1. Why did I choose (or was I chosen) to be at this workshop?

2. What talents, experience, skills, and knowledge do I bring to this day?

3. What do I know about the purpose of this workshop?

4. What do I expect will happen?

5. How will I know whether this day was valuable for me?

6. In what ways am I currently successful as an administrator or manager?

7. In what ways would I like to improve?

8. If I had this day "my way," how would I like it to be?

Thinking It Over

Having implemented Take a Page, what
surprised you about it?

_____

_____

_____

_____

_____

_____

What questions would you use again next time?

_____

_____

_____

_____

_____

What new questions would you ask?

_____

_____

_____

_____

_____

> By allowing participants to express
> their internal dialogue, I build rapport
> and buy-in.

HotTips for Facilitators ©2003 Zephyr Press • www.zephyrpress.com

Ask Two Powerful Questions

Use this technique to efficiently elicit people's visions for success and fears of failure for an organization or system.

For a facilitator, there is magic in the skill of asking provocative and thought-provoking questions. The following two questions are powerful openings to explore the positives and negatives of an organization, business, district, or school. We have also found them useful in meetings and task-force situations. In essence, you're facilitating the sharing of positive and negative scenarios associated with the organization. This accomplishes two things: (1) It allows people to speak from their experience, and (2) it allows emotions to be expressed in a productive way. The two powerful questions are

▶ **What are your best hopes?**
▶ **What are your worst fears?**

As simple as they seem, these two questions evoke a visible slice of the organization, business, or school, which empowers you as the facilitator to surface valuable information and begin building implementation strategies.

"What are your best hopes?" surfaces the group's vision for success. Through the dialogue, their collective desire for the kind of system or the school they want to become emerges. Many implementation strategies to reach this vision become clear as the list develops. The list becomes a "to-do" list. Each item becomes a goal or objective. As the wise facilitator that you are, you have now brought forth their best hopes and morphed each hope into a well-articulated goal with practical beginning steps. You have turned their dialogue into an action-oriented implementation plan. Congratulations!

"What are your worst fears?" evokes unresolved issues that must be probed for greater clarity. When carefully unveiled, they add realism and momentum to the process. Some of the fears we've heard are mistrust, not meeting deadlines, declining profits, diminishing test scores, employee dissention, and failure. How do you handle these? There are a couple of options. You can address each one in turn and elicit possible solutions. (This option works well when the fears have minimal emotional charge.) Alternatively, you might ask the group to prioritize the list from most damaging to least damaging, then work on solutions to the items the group is ready to handle. (This option allows participants to distance themselves from emotionally charged items as needed.) Addressing fears requires skill and tact. Venture into this area slowly, gently, and gracefully.

Making It Mine

Gather your team or associates. Work together through the following seven steps and discover what insights await you!

1. Each person takes a sheet of paper and folds it in half vertically, creating two long columns.

2. At the top of the left column, write the header "Best Hopes"; at the top of the right write "Worst Fears" (or "Challenges," for a more positive tone).

3. Invite each person quietly to write as many hopes and fears as possible. Allow about ten minutes. You can play soft baroque music in the background to increase focus.

4. Appoint one person as the scribe and a provide a large writing surface (a flip chart, a white board, an electronic board, an overhead, mural paper, or the like) on which to record all the hopes and fears. The scribe may write the items in traditional list format or use a different format such as mapping.

5. Go around the group, with each person contributing a response until all the hopes and fears have been recorded and are visible.

6. Allow five to ten minutes for discussion and clarification of any of the items on the lists.

7. Remind everyone that the intent of the process is to improve our system (or organization, team, workshop, or whatever). Explain that the group will take a short break, then begin focusing on the hopes; the fears will be addressed at the next scheduled meeting. From the "Best Hopes" list will emerge the beginnings of an implementation plan and first steps of action. Clarifying the goals first creates intention, purpose, and drive, which helps participants place the challenges in perspective and gain a deeper understanding of them.

Thinking It Over

What was the greatest benefit of the Ask Two Powerful Questions process?

_____

_____

_____

_____

_____

_____

_____

Where did the group get stuck? How did you facilitate them through the block?

Sticking point: _____

_____

_____

_____

_____

Facilitation: _____

_____

_____

_____

How would you modify the seven steps?

_____

_____

_____

_____

_____

_____

_____

_____

_____

> Ask Two Powerful Questions allows people to express their vision of success and barriers to it.

HotTips for Facilitators ©2003 Zephyr Press • www.zephyrpress.com

Do the "Now How"

Use this process to identify the steps necessary to implement a solution.

Have you ever noticed how groups, intent on solving a problem, often shy away from actual implementation? They can suggest great general solutions yet lose focus when detailing the steps for action. Doing the "Now How" is an excellent way to focus problem solvers on the details of implementation. The "Now How" process, once completed, becomes a blueprint for action.

Provide a large writing surface such as a chalkboard, white board, overhead, or the like. Guide the dialogue by stating or eliciting one desired outcome or solution and writing it on the left-hand side. Then ask, "Now How?" Encourage participants to respond with an action plan. Write these steps to the right in a decision-tree format.

For example, your group may be educators hoping to increase their school's academic performance index scores. You ask, "Now how?" Let's say the group generates three ideas to increase academic scores (see diagram on page 84). Now, for each of these ways, ask "Now How" again, to elicit means for accomplishing each idea. This branching process can continue until you reach an actual implementation plan.

ACADEMIC PERFORMANCE INDEX	Improve attendance: *"Now How?"*	rewards for attendance
		contact parents re: truancies
	Teach test-taking strategies: *"Now How?"*	mini-seminars
	Provide remediation: *"Now How?"*	after-school tutorials

"Now How" Steps

1. Agree on a goal and write it on the left side of a wide piece of paper.

2. Ask "Now How" to elicit ways to achieve the goal. Write each one on a branch coming off the goal.

3. Ask "Now How" again for each suggestion, resulting in additional branches with more detailed ideas.

4. Continue asking "Now How" for each detailed idea until the group has arrived at an implementation plan.

Making It Mine

Let's practice Doing the "Now How." Get a large sheet of paper and a pencil. Think of a goal you have for participants in your next event. Write it in a box on the left. List ways to achieve that outcome on lines to the right of the box. (See the diagram above for a model. Feel free to add as many lines as you need.) For each idea ask yourself again, "Now How?" Enjoy discovering solutions!

Thinking It Over

What benefits did I get from Doing the "Now How"?

_____
_____
_____
_____
_____
_____

What was unexpected about the process?

_____
_____
_____
_____
_____

What was reaffirming for me or the participants?

_____
_____
_____
_____
_____

> By asking "Now How?" I uncover the steps necessary to reach my desired outcomes.

Create Storyboards

Use structured visual displays for problem solving.

Storyboarding is an invention of Walt Disney's. In order to keep track of the thousands of drawings needed to achieve full animation of his cartoon features, Disney would have his artists pin their drawings in sequential order on the studio wall. From this big-picture view, he could quickly see which parts of a project were and were not complete. Storyboards have become commonly used among writers of feature movies, editors, and art directors, but they are not limited to artistic endeavors. We have used storyboards to conceptualize mission statements, develop best practices, and plan for improvements.

Personally, we think storyboarding is one of the best techniques for solving a complex problem. It is a creative and efficient structured brainstorming method for generating solutions to a seemingly overwhelming problem. The storyboard breaks the problem into smaller, more manageable parts and focuses attention on specific aspects of the problem. No other planning technique offers the same flexibility. It is an ideal way to share ideas and concepts, throwing them into a public arena for discussion and tapping the team's collective problem-solving capacity. It offers a flexible format that can easily be modified.

Here is the power of storyboards: Our experience shows that in a 60-minute non-storyboard brainstorming session with 14 participants, there might be about 40 to 45 responses. A storyboard session of the same size and time typically produces anywhere from 150 to 300 responses. In addition, our experience has been that in a typical brainstorming session, about a third of the participants produce 80% of the responses, another third give 20% of the responses, and the remaining participants act like observers of the meeting. In contrast, a storyboard session is fully participatory and places the entire sequence of a project, a company vision or policy, or a plan of action clearly in the hands of each participant, in clear sight of everyone in the room.

Materials Needed

✔ a stack of index cards
✔ marking pens
✔ tape
✔ colored $1/4$-inch press-on dots
✔ about 8 to 12 participants and a scribe
✔ a good deal of blank wall space

Procedure

At first, keep the process simple. As you become familiar and comfortable with the process, gradually explore more of its possibilities.

1. **Identify and define a problem:** Ask leading questions until the group agrees upon a main topic. Record it on an index card and place it at the top of the storyboard (see diagram on page 88).

2. **Generate ideas:** Have participants individually record on index cards their thoughts regarding the topic. They should write only one idea per card, the more ideas the better, and all ideas are accepted.

3. **Cluster the ideas:** Gather all the index cards, discuss each card with the group, and ask the group to cluster the cards by theme, similarities, and common features.

4. **Determine header cards:** Once three or four index cards have been clustered together, the group determines a heading that describes that cluster. Print the heading on an index card in bold red. Arrange the "cluster" index cards in a column underneath the header card.

5. **Prioritize:** Once all the cards have been discussed, clustered, and a heading for them determined, prioritize the headings on the storyboard. Give all the participants colored dots so they can prioritize their choices. They place their dots on whatever they feel are the most significant heading and subheading cards.

6. **Problem solve:** Take each cluster designated as a priority and generate solutions.

7. **Use for reference:** Keep the storyboard on the wall for group reference and further work. Also make copies for distribution to all participants.

The Problem

Header	Header	Header	Header

As the facilitator, remember the following pointers:

- Be unbiased.
- Create a pleasant, informal atmosphere.
- Lead the discussion to engage the group's creative energy.
- Provide positive feedback.
- Keep the process alive and moving.
- Ask clarifying questions.
- Encourage the group to self-manage their storyboard session.
- Induce curiosity.

We often wonder how a procedure so simple can possibly be so effective at unraveling complex issues. There is elegance in simplicity. It usually takes just one session to convince people of the richness of storyboards. The power they have to engage, stimulate, and unleash people's productivity is remarkable.

Making It Mine

Fill in the frame on page 90 to create your own storyboard.

Are you ready to take storyboards to a higher level? Explore these ideas:

- Train your colleagues and associates in this visual display technique.

- Provide your teams with issues to storyboard and offer them the flexibility to keep them posted as long as needed.

- Use storyboards for planning sessions to develop time lines and project assignments.

- Use the process to gain anonymous input from all meeting participants, especially during discussion of sensitive topics.

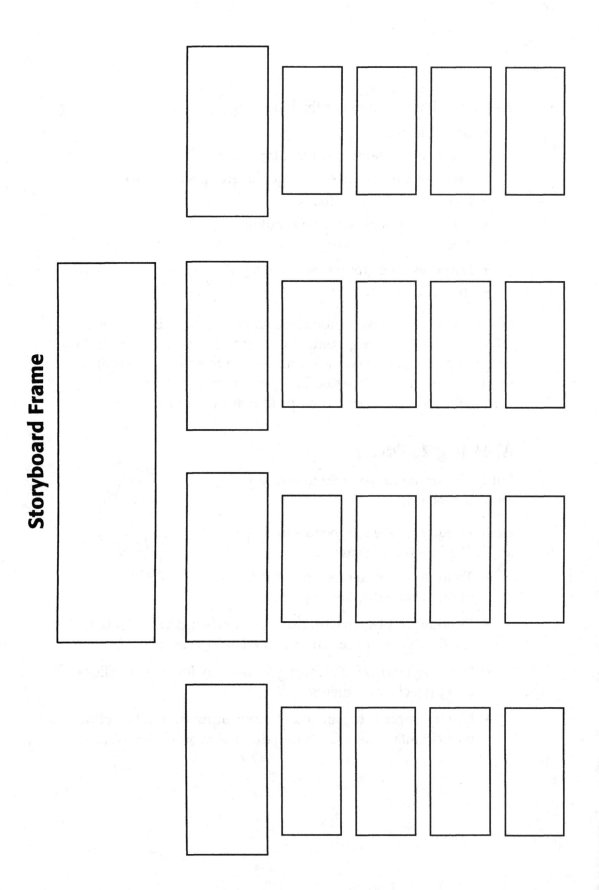

Storyboard Frame

Thinking It Over

What was the most significant benefit of storyboarding?

_____

_____

_____

_____

_____

_____

What other benefits did the storyboard offer me?

_____

_____

_____

_____

What will I do differently next time?

_____

_____

_____

_____

_____

> I unleash creativity and productivity when I Create Storyboards.

Ride the Brainstorm Carousel

Facilitate a stand-up, walk-around brainstorming session.

This HotTip is a classic. It gets participants up, moving, and talking. It allows small groups to hover around a chart or white board for a few minutes, brainstorm answers to a question, record their responses, and then move to another location and another chart to repeat the process. The bonus of the Brainstorm Carousel is that it requires minimal preparation.

Materials Needed

- ✔ flip charts or large sheets of paper and tape to make wall charts
- ✔ different colored markers
- ✔ clock or watch
- ✔ tape recorder and cassette with upbeat music (optional)

Procedure

1. Arrange about five sheets of paper at different locations on the walls or place five flip chart stands around the room. (Use more or less depending on the number of participants.) On each chart or sheet, write a question to answer or topic to respond to.

2. Organize participants into small groups, and give each group a different color of marker. Allow each group to choose a chart at which to start.

3. Each group goes to their chart and brainstorms ideas about the question or topic, recording their thoughts on the chart. (Remind your participants to write small enough that other groups can add to the same page.) Allow two minutes of brainstorming, after which the groups rotate clockwise to the next chart.

4. Each group reads the question and the responses recorded by previous groups, then adds their own responses at the bottom of the list. Once again, allow two minutes or so. Then signal the groups to move to the next chart and repeat the process.

5. We like to play upbeat "get-you-moving" music as the groups move from one chart to the next. Play the music until most participants have arrived at the new chart location and have begun reading the previous group's work recorded on the chart.

Making It Mine

We have provided a guide for generating your Brainstorm Carousel session. This gives you a chance to visualize how this process presents itself.

1. Consider the topic of your next facilitation. Think about the outcomes and your intent for the event.

2. With your desired outcome in mind, ask yourself, "What are the four to six most provocative, engaging, dialogue-prompting umbrella questions participants could answer about the topic?" For example, in a workshop called "Engage!" participants are greeted at the door with a passport. The passport outlines instructions for a Brainstorm Carousel. These questions are on the wall charts: What do you do when not in school? What metaphor do you use for teaching and learning? What do you hope your students

will learn from you this year? Why are you here? What and where do you teach? Other questions you might use are these: What are the characteristics of an effective leader? What does improvement look like for your department? If you could have professional development the way you wanted it, what would it be like?

3. Place your questions on the graphic on page 95.

Thinking It Over

What impact did Riding the Brainstorm Carousel have on my participants?

_____

_____

_____

What would have made the process go more smoothly?

_____

_____

_____

What other questions could I use in the future?

_____

_____

_____

> When I use the Brainstorm Carousel, I facilitate ideas, participation, and rapport.

Brainstorm Carousel Graphic

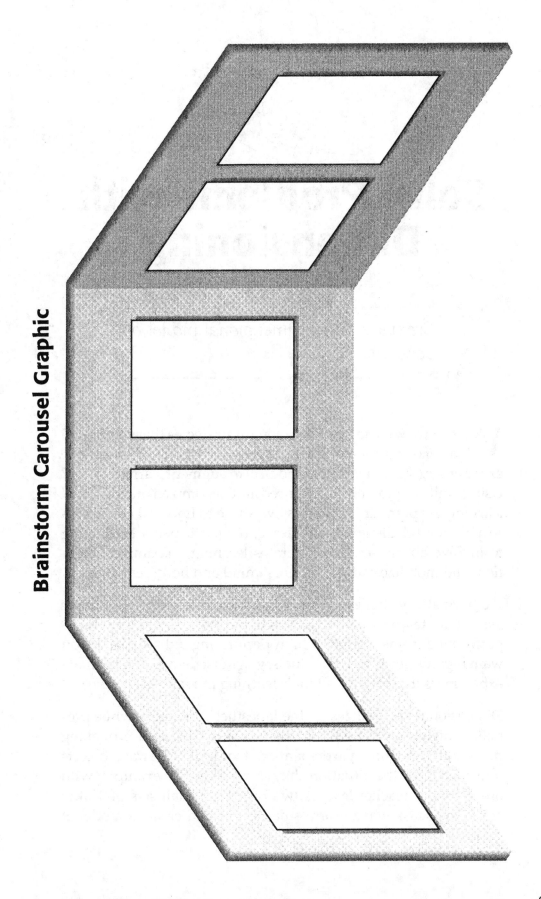

Solve Problems with Dimensioning

Create a three-dimensional model of a concept.

When we were teachers, we sought strategies that stimulated all of our students' senses, with special focus on kinesthetic experiences (that is, using their bodies) to augment learning. Why? Using multiple modalities enhanced and maximized our students' learning. As premier facilitators, we strive to find and create sensory-rich and challenging activities for our participants. Facilitating to involve all the senses accelerates learning, maximizes retention, and mobilizes all the learners' mind and body resources.

We have always believed that when we teach to the kinesthetic learner, we teach to all the learners in the room. If you want high-performing teams, you need high-performing individuals. If you want high-performing individuals, you must deliver and facilitate experiences that involve all their learning modalities.

Dimensioning capitalizes on the kinesthetic modality while propelling higher-order thinking. It is a creative, thought-provoking process that requires participants to manipulate various objects into models of the situation they are facing. For example, with one group of teacher-leaders, we provided small sets of Tinker Toys. Their task was to form small teams and create a model of effective coaching using the props. Intense dialogues were initiated as they creatively used the objects to render their collective vision of effective coaching in three dimensions.

Dimensioning interfaces creative thought and collective dialogue with physical movement. This physical process invites the participants to think by way of physical movement and manipulation. By using three-dimensional objects to create visual models, the dimensioning process offers new perspectives on the concept. Creating in several dimensions promotes seeing in several dimensions. This HotTip is facilitator heaven—fertile territory for "spinning out newness," where solutions, answers, innovations, new ideas, and paradigms reside. This is a great place to be when the goal is to achieve action and implementation.

Any props will do, so experiment with a variety of small manipulatives. Tinker Toys, Legos, small objects and shapes, marbles, Monopoly and other game pieces, small toy people, colored blocks and shapes, yo-yos, puzzles, pipe cleaners, or buttons are just a few ideas. Experiment, explore, and have fun.

Joel Barker, in his book *Future Edge* (1992), reminds us of a way to connect ourselves to the challenges of old paradigms and the sparks of new ones, a change known as a *paradigm shift*. Barker suggests we ask ourselves, "What do I believe is impossible to do in my business (or field, discipline, department, division, technology, or whatever)?" Then pair it with this question: "But what, if it could be done, would fundamentally change my business (or whatever)?" Considering the "impossible" takes you outside your boundaries, and "fundamentally" suggests the level of change needed. When we combine these two attributes, we begin shifting our paradigms.

Making It Mine

Make this HotTip yours through a personal paradigm-dimensioning project we have designed just for you.

Place in front of you several office supplies, such as a pen, a pencil, a glue stick, an eraser, a bottle of correction fluid, tape, a pad of sticky notes, a stapler, paper clips, scissors, a hole puncher. Ask a colleague to be your partner for conversation.

Choose an area of focus: your business, your department, your school, your job or position, the economy, or whatever you deem important to you. Now ask yourself the paradigm question: "What is impossible for me to do in _____ (your focus area) but, if it could be done, would fundamentally change the way I _____?"

1. Using the props to symbolize actual people and issues in your focus area, begin to tell a story about your paradigm shift.

2. Choose an object to represent yourself and explain why you chose that object. Name specific ways you and the object are similar. Now incorporate that object into your model.

3. Next, choose objects that best represent some of the impossibilities. What is it about the characteristics of those objects that are similar to the impossibilities you face? Place those objects in your model.

4. For each object that represents an impossibility, choose another object that would represent the fundamental change. For example, if I chose a glue stick to represent the lack of flexibility that impedes communication in my current system, I might then choose a highlighter to represent the fundamental change of highlighting the need for structured communication protocols.

5. Continuing to use the props as metaphoric symbols, turn each of your impossibilities into words and thoughts of action toward a fundamental change.

6. Reflect on any insights you gained as a result of the activity. Based on your insights from this activity, what new behaviors might you start working on?

Here are a few other questions for you to ask yourself:

- What is impossible for me to do as a facilitator but, if I could do it, would fundamentally change the way I facilitate?

- What is impossible to do as a leader . . . ?

- What is impossible to do as a colleague . . . ?

- What is impossible to do as a friend . . . ?

- What is impossible to do as a spouse . . . ?

- What is impossible to do spiritually . . . ?

- What is impossible to do in this relationship . . . ?

Thinking It Over

What value have I gained from this experience?

_____

_____

_____

_____

_____

How could I use Dimensioning in my next meeting or event?

_____

_____

_____

_____

_____

_____

What props will I choose for that purpose?

_____

_____

_____

_____

_____

_____

_____

_____

> **Considering the impossible as possible opens the way for creative options.**

Part 3

Use the Classics

What follows are three of our tried-and-true activities for team building and revealing participants' potential. Build a Tower and Build a Roller Coaster have participants create and test a team product. Both activities limit the number and kind of supplies available and provide excellent opportunities to employ Ride the Winds of Fate (see page 36). Draw It reveals the hidden artist in each of us and shows participants that they can do more than they realized they could.

Because these are group activities rather than facilitator strategies, we have presented the information in a different format than the other HotTips to facilitate implementation. For all three activities, we provide goals, time, materials, and procedures. We've also included sample debriefing questions, which invite participants to explore their experience, draw conclusions about their interpersonal and intrapersonal abilities, and apply these insights to their work and their lives.

We pass these activities on to you knowing the impact they have had on our participants. We have personally tested these three classics with a variety of audiences and ages. Feel free to modify them to meet your own training needs.

Build a Tower

Use this simulation to create an inclusive, nonverbal, energizing, collaborative experience.

This classic activity is a great energizer that creates a sense of inclusion among team members. It's a good way for participants to experience working together in a positive, nonverbal manner. It can help a team develop closer working relationships. For a team experiencing communication challenges, this activity can support their understanding of the issues by highlighting the conflicts and where change is needed. It also provides a team-building experience that helps the team come together to collaborate and create.

Goals

- To build teamwork (mutual support, cohesiveness, and synergy)
- To promote awareness of issues influencing team effectiveness
- To explore nonverbal communication

Time Required

45–60 minutes (can be flexible depending on outcome)

Materials

✔ 30–50 sheets of 8¹/₂″ x 11″ paper per team
✔ 1–2 rolls of masking tape per team
✔ Markers (optional for added creativity)

Groupings

Small groups of 4–8 people per group

Instructions

1. Form groups of four to eight participants each.
2. Distribute paper, masking tape, and markers.
3. Explain that each group's task is to construct a tower within a specific amount of time using only the given materials and communicating only nonverbally.
4. State the time frame. At the end of the specified time, stop the building process.
5. Have all groups circulate to view and acknowledge the work of the other teams.
6. Bring all the teams together for discussion and reflection, using the following debriefing questions as a guide.

Debriefing Questions

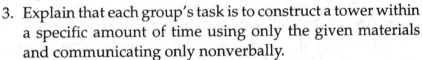

• Did you have enough materials and time?
• Would more or less of either have been helpful?
• What does it take for team projects to work well?
• What was happening in your group?
• What was difficult about not talking to one another?

- How would the task have been different if you had been able to talk to one another?
- Who started the building?
- Did leaders emerge?
- Did any people just give up?
- Were you aware of the feelings of your other group members?
- What was the best thing that happened?
- What made you feel good? Frustrated? Sad?
- What nonverbal signals were people giving one another regarding either the building of the structure or their feelings?
- How did you decide as a team what to do?
- What is the biggest lesson you learned in doing this task?
- What did you learn about yourself?
- During this activity, did you use your usual style of working with others?
- Are you an effective team member?
- How might you change the way you built your structure if you could do this activity over again?

Build a
Roller Coaster

Enhance planning skills, problem solving, collaboration, and time management with this simulation activity.

In this simulation, your participants, working in teams, design and build the last section of a paper roller coaster.

Goals

- To promote teamwork
- To improve time management
- To increase presentation skills
- To challenge problem-solving skills

Time Required

30–45 minutes for planning and construction, plus about 15 minutes for trial runs and debriefing (time can be flexible)

Materials

✔ Marbles
✔ Rolls of adding machine paper (usually used for the tracks)
✔ paper clips
✔ scissors
✔ masking tape
✔ rulers
✔ wooden craft sticks
✔ pipe cleaners
✔ paper cups (various sizes)
✔ any other materials you think of that could be used

Groupings

Group the participants into construction-company teams of 4–10 participants.

Instructions

1. Explain that each group represents a construction company. Each company has had past success in building exciting roller coasters that are safe and thrilling and possess that extra bit of flair and imagination.

2. The group's task is to design the final section of a roller coaster. To add interest, you might say, "We invite each team to participate in this unusual yet challenging event—to design and construct the final section of a roller coaster using the supplies provided. We hope you will find the task enjoyable, challenging, and valuable."

3. Present the specifications the groups must meet (see page 107). It may be helpful to post these where the groups can refer to them as they work.

4. Explain that each team's success will be judged by having them demonstrate their roller coaster by rolling a marble down it. Emphasize that in judging you will consider the quality of the group's teamwork, the originality of the design, and the dynamism with which the group presents the final product. For example, you might say

---

As the facilitator, I will look favorably on imaginative features, thrills, variety, and an exciting finish. I will also observe the way you work as a team and may come around to ask you questions while your team is designing and building. I will be impressed by a dynamic presentation, perhaps mentioning the problems and difficulties encountered. I will be less enthusiastic if your team says nothing and simply drops a marble at the top of the coaster.

Specifications

1. The track must include at least one uphill section.
2. The track may be straight, curved, or both.
3. The track must be free-standing with no human support.
4. The release point of the car (marble) must be at the top of the track.
5. When demonstrating and presenting your model, you will be allowed three runs of the marble.

Debriefing Questions

- How did your group begin?
- Did you start by working independently?
- Did you have a brainstorming session?
- Did you start by discussing options?
- Did you consider the time factor?
- Looking back, did you devote too much time to one aspect?

- Did you consider how to present your roller coaster?
- Did you assign different jobs within your team?
- Did you appoint a group leader?
- Did you put someone in charge of keeping time?
- How did you handle disagreements?
- Did you build from plans or just start building?
- Did you have engineering difficulties?
- What types of construction did you consider but reject?
- How did you cope with stress in the final minutes before the deadline?
- How effective were your communication and decision-making skills?
- Did one person do most of the work, or was the effort divided among the team members?
- What were some problems, and how did you find solutions to them?
- Did you discuss who could work well with their hands?
- What are your final thoughts about this challenging activity?

Draw It

Produce impressive success in drawing with this experiential activity.

This classic is a little different yet usually produces many insights among the participants. Most participants experience drawing success beyond their expectations.

Goals

- To understand and experience strategies for gaining access to the visual, perceptive mode of the brain
- To allow participants to experience their hidden drawing potential as a confidence builder
- To provide a positive anchor experience that leads participants from lack of confidence to success
- To experience seeing challenges from alternative viewpoints as a way to find new solutions and solve complex scenarios
- To gain increased trust in one's abilities
- To experience an opportunity to Pause, Be Silent, and Attend (page 49)
- To understand that drawing is a global skill requiring only a limited set of basic components

Time Required

A total of 45 to 75 minutes, divided as follows:

1. Introduction to the activity: 10 minutes
2. Setting up ground rules for the drawing process: 5 minutes
3. Modeling the process for participants: 5 minutes
4. Drawing time: 20–40 minutes (flexible)
5. Debriefing and discussion: 5–15 minutes

It will also be to your advantage to practice the process a few times before presenting it to a group, so you can model it proficiently.

Materials

✔ plenty of sheets of white drawing paper
✔ sharpened pencils with erasers for each person
✔ chart pad and easel for facilitator modeling
✔ simple line illustrations or cartoons for each participant to copy—our favorite is Donald Duck (enough that all participants can draw the same illustration at first, plus some alternatives so they can try a different illustration if they wish)
✔ music to draw by

Groupings

This is an intrapersonal process and activity. Each participant draws alone in his or her own quiet spot. The actual drawing time becomes very relaxing, peaceful, and refreshing.

Instructions

1. Begin by providing background information and encouragement:

The ability to draw depends on the ability to see the way an artist sees. You will soon discover that drawing is a skill that can be learned by every person with average eyesight and eye-hand coordination. If your handwriting is readable, or if you can print legibly, you have ample dexterity to draw well. The key to the mystery of drawing is an ability to access a different way of seeing and perceiving. When you learn to see in the special way that experienced artists do, then you can draw.

---

2. Explain that participants will copy a master illustration by turning it upside down so as to confuse the brain into seeing only lines and shapes rather than the actual objects. Participants should draw the outside lines first, then the interior lines. Remind them to draw exactly the lines and shapes they see, without trying to make sense of the picture. Turning the picture upside down will support them in doing so.

3. Explain that when it is time to begin drawing, you will ask each participant to find a quiet spot. They should not talk during the drawing experience, letting drawing be their language. Also explain that you will play music during the drawing time to stimulate the brain and enhance the learning environment.

4. After you have set the context and rules for the process, reinforce those rules by modeling exactly what the drawing process will look, sound, and feel like. Using the easel and chart paper, model drawing the master illustration while everyone watches. Turn on the music during this time, to encourage the participants to watch quietly and respect

the learning environment. Remember to turn the drawing upside down, duplicate the lines and shapes as closely as possible, and begin with the outline before filling in the inner lines. (It is wise to practice this step a few times before presenting it to the entire group, so you can present an effective model of the experience.)

5. Pass out pencils, paper, and a master illustration to each participant. (All participants should receive the same master illustration.)

6. Invite participants to have fun, enjoy, relax, and be amazed at how well they can draw.

Debriefing Questions

- How many of you felt that you drew better than you have ever drawn before?

- What was your concept of the passage of time? Did the time go by quickly? Slowly?

- How did you feel while you were in this resourceful brain state for drawing?

- How much confidence did you have in your drawing ability before? What about now?

- Was this difficult for anyone? Why?

- Who was amazed at how well they actually drew?

- What made this activity fun and challenging?

- Having completed this activity, what can you say about how you might approach challenges in your life?

Part 4

Closing and Reflection

We often learn best after the fact, from reflecting on our experiences. Remember that the brain is a pattern-seeking, meaning-making, purpose-detecting organ diligently employing its resources to make sense of our experiences. Given the time constraints of our jobs, workshops, and trainings we often neglect the essential need for reflection, the white space required to make the text of our thinking stand out. We offer two tips, Debrief Their Learning and Walk About as structures that surface and capture the brilliance arising from reflection.

Debrief Their Learning

Facilitate the closing of a learning activity
with these simple debriefing guidelines.

Your participants have just completed an amazing activity. They are excited and appreciative of the experience. Now what? Move on to the next activity? Take a break? Not yet. Maximize their experience by facilitating an equally amazing debriefing session.

Debrief Their Learning is an activity that usually happens at the end of a simulation experience, meeting, or workshop. It helps participants reflect on their learning experience, relate new learnings to their worldview, and discover insights. Debriefing helps you bring closure to the process by bringing forth salient highlights and distinctions.

The intent of Debrief Their Learning is to allow insights to build on each other and to deepen everyone's perception of the meaning of the experience. When facilitating this session, it is important to balance spontaneity with structure (the following list we invite you to try). Please view our five phases and corresponding questions as flexible suggestions rather than rigid requirements. Please feel free to rearrange or delete phases to meet your needs and the available time. If the conversation drifts from one phase to another, then returns to the previous phase, roll with it. As long as the salient points are covered, you have achieved your purpose.

Phase 1: How was the experience?

During this phase, ask how participants felt about the activity. You might ask them how they felt at different points during the event, how they felt about their level of participation, and how they felt about the overall process. This is also a good opportunity to ask participants about their feelings toward other participants, their small group, and other groups.

Phase 2: What happened?

During the second phase, ask about what happened. Ask them to recall important things that occurred during the course of the process. You can ask them to list various events chronologically or by importance.

Phase 3: What did you learn?

In the third phase, ask questions about what participants learned. Invite them to come up with several principles they discovered through the experience (teamwork, continual improvement, apparent failures that turn out to be successes on deeper analysis). Ask them to recall specific actions and comments to support or refute each principle proposed.

Phase 4: What connections can you make?

In this phase, invite participants to dialogue about the relevance of the simulation to their workplace and daily experiences. Ask such questions as, "How does this relate to the real world?" or, "How does this simulation reflect events in your workplace?" Suggest that participants view the simulation as a metaphor and speculate on what workplace event is captured by the metaphor. Identify the components of the simulation and ask participants to name similar experiences from their workplace.

Phase 5: What's next?

This is the action plan phase. Encourage participants to apply their insights to new contexts. Specifically, discuss how they would apply what they have learned to their workplace. Ask how they would change their strategies if they were to play the simulation again, knowing what they know now. Ask participants how their workplace behaviors would change as a result of the insights gained from the simulation game.

Making It Mine

Create a debriefing guide and an archive of exemplary debriefing questions. Using the preceding guidelines as a template, begin to create your personal debriefing guide. Base your guide on two strategies. The first is an analysis of the simulation and the model of reality it incorporates. The second is the application of the simulation to participants' lives. Personal experience will offer one of the best sources for creating your guide. Turn what you have learned in past facilitations into provocative questions to add to your archive. Invite others to assist in analyzing the content and metaphoric principles. Recall spontaneous comments and questions from previous debriefing sessions. This information will add significant ideas and questions for your guide. Remember to improve your guide each time you learn something new from facilitating a debriefing session.

Thinking It Over

What are the most useful questions I ask? How do I know they are valuable?

_____

_____

_____

_____

_____

_____

_____

_____

_____

_____

_____

In the debriefing process, where do participants get stuck? What question would move them forward?

Sticking point: _____

_____

_____

Question: _____

_____

_____

What are two qualities I want to remember to exhibit during the next debriefing session?

1. _____

_____

_____

2. _____

_____

_____

> **Debrief Their Learning adds punch to the salient points and embeds them in participants' memories.**

Walk about to Facilitate Reflection and Growth

Use this peer- and self-coaching process to identify ways to improve your next facilitation experience.

As we navigate the waters of innovation, we are faced with challenges: How do we design and facilitate sensory-rich, challenging experiences for our participants? How do we encourage them to take responsibility for their learning while ensuring that they meet or exceed standards or benchmarks? How do we accelerate understanding and retention while fostering transfer? These are big questions that require us to consider what we do, how we do it, and how what we do affects our participants.

This guided reflection and growth process involves you and your colleagues in posing provocative questions about how you can improve and accelerate your ability to create quality educational experiences. Although this process can be completed individually, it is far more powerful in trios, so grab a couple of colleagues and go for it! One person at a time completes the activity by answering a set of six questions. The other two people listen and observe their colleague's nonverbal signals, posture, gestures, pitch, tone, tempo, and volume.

The Process

1. Choose six different locations in your room for a Walk About path. You will answer one question in each location.
2. Recall a lesson or training you designed and delivered or a meeting you conducted.
3. With this situation in mind, move to each location on the path in turn and answer one of the six questions that follow.
4. Debrief in an area away from the Walk About path, using the debriefing questions.

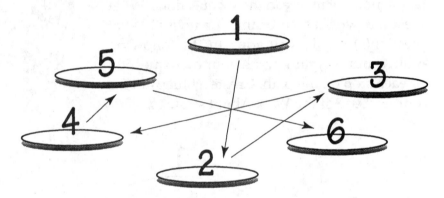

The Questions

1. What was your desired outcome? Was it met? How do you know?
2. What did you hope would be different in your participants' lives as a result of the lesson or training? How would you know whether that change occurred?
3. What feedback would supportive participants give you about the strengths of your lesson or training?
4. What feedback would critical participants' give you about the shortcomings of your lesson or training?
5. What advice would a coach, mentor, or master teacher offer you about your lesson or training?
6. What changes would you make next time? How might you implement those changes?

Debriefing Questions

1. What insights did you gain?
2. At which location or locations in the Walk About did you gain them?
3. What will you do with the insights you've gained?

Making It Mine

Take a moment to reread the six questions. What questions would you change or revise? What question(s) would you add? In the following Walk About diagram, write your own question for each stop on the path. Create a blueprint for your next use of the Walk About strategy.

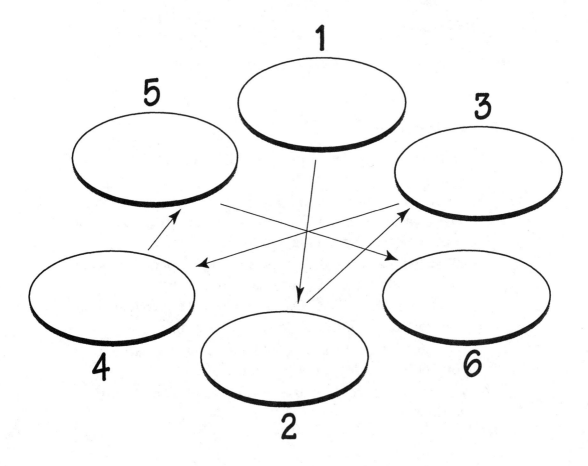

Thinking It Over

Imagine a lesson or training you've delivered. Feel the impact of each question as you reflect on what you and your participants said and did. Having now experienced this process, how might you implement the insights you've gained?

_____

_____

_____

_____

What was most beneficial about the Walk About experience? How do you know?

_____

_____

_____

_____

What will you do differently next time you use this strategy?

_____

_____

_____

_____

Each time I facilitate reflection, I facilitate change.

Possible Answers for
Every Body Tells a Story

These are our suggestions for possible meanings of the behavioral signs on page 53. Remember, there are several reasonable interpretations of these signs, so if you have some different answers, do not assume they are incorrect.

Flared nostrils: heightened negative emotions; distaste or fear

Blinking: attempting to understand, to "see" a concept more clearly

Leaning forward: interest, attentiveness

Change of face color: flushed = heightened attention on self; pale = deepened reflection and personal connection

Rapid breathing: if from upper chest, visual processing

Eye contact: interest, attentiveness; preparing to break in or ask a question

Large hand gestures: using kinesthetic modality

Bent posture: anticipation

Smiling expression: enjoyment

No expression: visual or auditory processing (flat affect); boredom

Rapid movements: excitement or discomfort

Moist hands: heightened anxiety

Closed fist: hanging on to a thought, idea, belief

Crossed arms: considering a key point; defensiveness; feeling cold

Higher than usual vocal pitch: enthusiasm or uncertainty; nervousness

Rapid speech: enthusiasm or uncertainty; nervousness

Further Learning

Abernathy, Rob, and Mark Reardon. 2002. *HotTips for Speakers: 25 Surefire Ways to Engage and Captivate Any Group or Audience*. Tucson, Ariz.: Zephyr Press.

————. 2002. *HotTips for Teachers: 30+ Steps to Student Engagement*. Tucson, Ariz.: Zephyr Press.

Armstrong, Thomas. 1993. *Seven Kinds of Smart*. New York: Penguin Books.

Barker, Joel A. 1992. *Future Edge: Discovering the New Paradigms of Success*. New York: William Morrow.

Block, Peter. 1993. *Stewardship: Choosing Service over Self-Interest*. San Francisco, Calif.: Berrett-Koehler Publishers.

Caine, Renate N., and Geoffrey Caine. 1994. *Making Connections: Teaching and the Human Brain*. Menlo Park, Calif.: Addison-Wesley.

————. 1997. *Education on the Edge of Possibility*. Alexandria, Va.: Association of Supervision and Curriculum Development.

Campbell, Don G. 1992. *100 Ways to Improve Teaching Using Your Voice and Music: Pathways to Accelerate Learning*. Tucson, Ariz.: Zephyr Press.

Chawla, Sarita, and John Renesch, eds. 1994. *Learning Organizations: Developing Cultures for Tomorrow's Workplace*. Portland, Ore.: Productivity Press.

Costa, Arthur, and Robert Garmston. 1994. *Cognitive Coaching: A Foundation for Renaissance Schools*. Norwood, Mass.: Christopher-Gordon Publishers.

DePorter, Bobbi. 1992. *Quantum Learning*. New York: Dell.

DePorter, Bobbi, Sarah Singer-Nourie, and Mark Reardon. 1999. *Quantum Teaching: Orchestrating Student Success*. Needham Heights, Mass.: Allyn and Bacon.

Doyle, Michael, and David Strauss. 1993. *How to Make Meetings Work: The New Interaction Method*. New York: Berkeley Books.

Ewing, I. 1994. *The Best Presentation Skills*. Singapore: Ewing Communications.

Fripp, Patricia. 1995. *You've Got to Be Lively: Speaking Secrets of the Masters*. Harrisburg, Pa.: Executive Books.

Fullan, Michael. 1993. *Change Forces: Probing the Depth of Educational Reform*. London and New York: Falmer Press.

Gardner, Howard. 1993. *Frames of Mind*. 2nd. ed. New York: Basic Books.

Garmston, Robert J., and Bruce M. Wellman. 1992. *How to Make Presentations That Teach and Transform*. Alexandria, Va.: Association for Supervision and Curriculum Development.

————. 1995. Adaptive Schools in a Quantum Universe. *Educational Leadership* 52 (7): 6–12

Goleman, Daniel. 1995. *Emotional Intelligence.* New York: Bantam Books.

Guskey, Thomas R. 1995. Results-Oriented Professional Development: In Search of an Optimal Mix of Effective Practices. *Journal of Staff Development* 15 (fall).

Harmin, Merrill. 1995. *Inspiring Active Learning.* Edwardsville, Ill.: Inspiring Strategies Institute.

Hart, Leslie. 1983. *Human Brain, Human Learning.* New York: Brain Age Publishers.

Jensen, Eric. 1994. *The Learning Brain.* Del Mar, Calif.: Turning Point.

————. 1996. *The Brain-Based Approach.* Del Mar, Calif.: Turning Point.

Killion, J., and L. Simmons. 1992. The Zen of Facilitation. *Journal of Staff Development* 13 (3).

Kofman, F., and Peter M. Senge. 1993. Communities of Commitment: The Heart of Learning Organizations. *Organizational Dynamics* Autumn: 5–23.

Margulies, Nancy, with Nusa Maal. 2001. *Mapping Inner Space: Learning and Teaching Visual Mapping.* 2nd. ed. Tucson, Ariz.: Zephyr Press.

Nickerson, S. 1995. Breaking the Language Barrier. *Training and Development Journal* 49 (2): 45–48.

Rico, Gabriele. n.d. *One-Pagers: Creating Patterns of Knowing.* Spring, Tex.: Absey & Co., forthcoming.

Rose, Colin, and Malcolm Nicholl. 1997. *Accelerated Learning for the Twenty-First Century.* New York: Delacorte Press.

Scholnick, Ellin K., Katherine Nelson, Susan A. Gelman, and Patricia H. Miller, eds. 1999. *Conceptual Development: Piaget's Legacy.* Jean Piaget Symposium series. Mahwah, N.J.: Lawrence Erlbaum Associates.

Senge, Peter M. 1990. *The Fifth Discipline: The Art and Practice of the Learning Organization.* New York: Doubleday.

Sylwester, Robert. 1995. *A Celebration of Neurons.* Alexandria, Va.: Association of Supervision and Curriculum Development.

True, H. 1995. *The Power of Humor: Speaking Secrets of the Masters.* Harrisburg, Pa.: Executive Books.

Wheatley, Margaret J. 1999. *Leadership and the New Science.* 2nd. ed. San Francisco, Calif.: Berrett-Koehler Publishers.